Doing Justice
The Choice of Punishments

Doing Justice

The Choice of Punishments

ANDREW VON HIRSCH

*Report of the Committee for the
Study of Incarceration*

Preface by
CHARLES E. GOODELL, *Chairman*

Introduction by
WILLARD GAYLIN *and*
DAVID J. ROTHMAN

HILL AND WANG · NEW YORK
A division of Farrar, Straus and Giroux

Published simultaneously in Canada
by McGraw-Hill Ryerson Ltd., Toronto

Printed in the United States of America

First edition, 1976

Designed by Gustave Niles

Library of Congress Cataloging in Publication Data

Von Hirsch, Andrew.
  Doing justice.

  "Additional views of individual committee members"
  Includes bibliographical references and index.
  1. Prison sentences. 2. Rehabilitation of criminals.
3. Recidivists. 4. Punishment. I. Committee for the
Study of Incarceration. II. Title.
HV8708.V65   364.6'1   75-35882

Acknowledgments

THE Committee's work, and this book, were made possible through generous grants from the Field Foundation and the New World Foundation. We also wish to thank the Lawyers' Committee for Civil Rights Under Law, which provided office space for the project and which administered the project's funds. The opinions expressed, however, are our own and do not necessarily represent those of the Lawyers' Committee.

We are greatly indebted to our professional staff: to David F. Greenberg, whose ideas and research papers much influenced our thinking; to Susan Steward, for her able research and her suggestions on the strategy of the argument; and to Patricia Ebener and Andrea Shechter for their work on background data and footnotes. We also thank

Richard A. Tropp, who served as our consultant at the inception of the project.

We are grateful to our patient and skillful secretaries, Janiska Boudreau, Stephany Brown, and Martha Ann Richardson, who had to type the innumerable memoranda and drafts that led to this book.

We thank Dr. Benjamin F. Payton, Officer in Charge of Higher Education and Minority Affairs at the Ford Foundation, who participated as a member during the first year of the project until the press of other duties required him to withdraw.

Most of all, we wish to acknowledge our debt to Harry Kalven, Jr., Harry A. Bigelow Professor of Law at the University of Chicago, who was a member of our Committee until his death last year. His thinking was critical to the shaping of our argument, and this book is dedicated to him.

The Committee for the Study of Incarceration

THE COMMITTEE

Commission of Correction; Professor of Law at the State University of New York at Buffalo (on leave).

STANTON WHEELER, Professor of Law and Sociology at Yale Law School. Co-author of *Socialization after Childhood*.

LESLIE T. WILKINS, Professor of Criminal Justice at the State University of New York at Albany. Author of *Evaluation of Penal Measures*.

THE STAFF

ANDREW VON HIRSCH, Executive Director and principal author of this report. During 1974–5, the final year of the project, he was Visiting Associate Professor of Criminal Justice at the State University of New York at Albany. He is now Associate Professor of Criminal Justice at Rutgers University, and Senior Research Associate at the Center for Policy Research.

DAVID F. GREENBERG, Senior Fellow (through May 1973). Dr. Greenberg was one of the principal authors of the American Friends Service Committee's report, *Struggle for Justice*. He is now Assistant Professor of Sociology at New York University.

SUSAN STEWARD, Research associate. Ms. Steward is now an attorney with the Office of General Counsel of the Department of Health, Education and Welfare, Washington, D.C.

PATRICIA EBENER, Research assistant (through October 1972).

ANDREA SHECHTER, Research aide.

JANISKA BOUDREAU, Secretary.

Contents

Preface
by CHARLES E. GOODELL   xv

Introduction
by WILLARD GAYLIN *and* DAVID J. ROTHMAN   xxi

1
Dimensions of the Study   3

I
The Conventional Assumptions   9

2
The Rehabilitative Disposition   11

3
Predictive Restraint   19

4
"Individualization"   27

II
Why Punish at All?
—The General Justification of Punishment   35

5
General Deterrence   37

6
Desert   45

III
How Severely to Punish?
—The Allocation of Penalties   59

7
Deterrence and Allocation   61

8
The Principle of Commensurate Deserts   66

9
Seriousness of Crimes   77

10
Prior Criminal Record   84

11
Severity of Punishments   89

IV
Toward a Sentencing System   97

12
Discretion and Sentencing Standards   98

13
Incarceration   107

14
Alternatives to Incarceration   118

15

Variations from the Deserved Sentence:
What If One Could Predict or Rehabilitate? 124

16
Arraying Penalties on a Scale 132

V
Lingering Questions 143

17
Just Deserts in an Unjust Society 143

Notes 151

Appendix
Additional Views of Individual Committee Members 171

Preface

IN EARLY 1971, the Field Foundation asked me to chair this study. There was growing disenchantment with prisons, and with the disparities and irrationalities of the sentencing process. Yet reformers lacked a rationale to guide them in their quest for alternatives, save for the more-than-century-old notion of rehabilitation that had nurtured the rise of the penitentiary. The purpose of our study was to consider afresh the fundamental concepts concerning what is to be done with the offender after conviction. The members of the Committee were chosen from a wide variety of disciplines, extending well beyond traditional correctional specialties. The project was staffed and organized during the spring and summer of 1971, and began its deliberations that fall.

This book is the product of the Committee's work over a

four-year period, during which more than twenty working sessions were held. The conclusions herein represent the thinking of the group as it emerged in these discussions. All the members of the Committee subscribe to the report: that is, they support, on balance, its contentions (although not all of them necessarily agree with every conclusion, recommendation, or emphasis). A few of the members have furnished individual statements in the Appendix, noting additional thoughts or reservations.

We were aware that, in committee writings, coherence of argument can too easily be lost in the effort to accommodate divergent viewpoints. To avoid that pitfall, we charged one person with the task of weaving together into a single argument the different thoughts emerging in our discussions. We chose for that task our Executive Director, Andrew von Hirsch—who had already played a crucial role in our deliberations, both in innovating ideas for us to consider and in pressing us to refine our own thinking. In the writing task, he continued his dual function—as he both incorporated the themes of our discussions into the book and put his own philosophical stamp on the product in synthesizing them into a unified framework of ideas.

What emerges from our study is a conceptual model that differs considerably from the dominant thinking about punishment during this century. The conventional wisdom has been that the sentence should be fashioned so as to rehabilitate the offender and isolate him from society if he is dangerous. To accomplish that, the sentencer was to be given the widest discretion to suit the disposition to the particular criminal. For reasons which this book explains, we reject these notions as unworkable and unjust. We conclude that the severity of the sentence should depend on the seriousness of the defendant's crime or crimes—on what he *did* rather than on what the sentencer expects he will do if treated in a certain fashion.

From our conceptual model, there follow a number of important reforms which I might note briefly:

· Stringent limitation on incarceration as punishment. Only offenders convicted of serious offenses would be confined. Even for such offenders, the duration of confinement would be strictly rationed: instead of the ten-, fifteen-, and twenty-year sentences now imposed, we would allow very few sentences exceeding three years.

· Alternatives to incarceration for the bulk of criminal offenses—namely, for those which do not qualify as serious. These alternatives would not be rehabilitative measures but, simply and explicitly, less severe punishments. Warnings, limited deprivations of leisure time, and, perhaps, fines would be used in lieu of imprisonment.

· Sharply scaled-down penalties for first offenders. The sentence would depend not only on the seriousness of the crime of which the defendant now stands convicted but also on his record of prior offenses. Where there were no prior convictions, the sentence would be diminished substantially (except for the very serious crimes).

· Reduction in sentencing disparity. Offenders with similar criminal histories would receive similar punishments.

· Narrowing of sentencing discretion. The wide, uncharted discretionary leeway which sentencing judges now enjoy—and which contributes so much to disparity of sentence—would be discontinued. Instead, sentencing guidelines would be established that prescribe standardized

penalties for offenses of different degrees of seriousness
(with a limited amount of variation permitted for aggravating and mitigating circumstances).

• Elimination of indeterminacy of sentence. Now, when a
defendant is sentenced to prison, he has no idea how long
he will stay. That is decided at an indefinite future date by a
parole board, which is supposedly expert in telling how well
he is "adjusting." The uncertainty of the release date has
been one of the worst agonies of prison life—with prisoners
kept for years in suspense as to when they may finally leave.
In our theory, there is no need for indeterminacy, as the
sentence is to be based on the seriousness of the defendant's
past offense or offenses—and that is knowable at the time of
conviction. In the instances when an offender is to be
confined, he will at least know for how long.

To THIS BOOK's arguments and conclusions—which, I think,
speak for themselves—I might add one observation of my
own. It is possible, I believe, to create a fairer and less
brutal penal system. Disparity can be reduced, intelligible
standards for sentencing can be formulated, and severe
punishments can be strictly limited. What I do not think is a
feasible goal, however, is to "solve the crime problem" by
tinkering with penal methods. It is a strength of this report,
I believe, that it offers its suggested reforms as a means of
making the system fairer.

It does not offer illusory promises of eradicating crime, as
reformers too often have done in the past.

It is surely an understatement that there is too much
crime in this society and that crime causes terrible suffering.
The criminal sanction, however, is a quite limited tool, and

we should do well to remember its limitations. Judging from my own observations and from what I have learned in the course of this project, I doubt that changes in the sentencing and correctional system can work a dramatic reduction in crime rates. However enlightened or ingenious our penal methods become, this country probably will long be condemned to suffer the high crime rates now in evidence—given our history of domestic violence and the extent of disparities in wealth and social status. Certainly, the evidence does not suggest that further increases in the already inflated penalty levels will make a dent in today's crime rates. In increasing penalties—in order to appease our frustrations that previous increases didn't "solve the problem"—we long ago reached the point of diminishing returns. There are, as this book points out, important moral objections to any further inflation of penalties; in fact, a substantial deflation is essential as a matter of justice.

Today we have not only rampant crime but a gruesome system of punishment: harsh, arbitrary, and lacking in coherent rationale. The latter, at least, we can try to change. We can mitigate severities of punishment to levels more consistent with our pretenses of being a civilized society, and we can have some intelligible conception of why we are punishing. We can, I am convinced, mitigate the harshness and caprice of the penal system without losing whatever usefulness in crime prevention it now has. If we could accomplish this much, it would be no mean achievement.

CHARLES E. GOODELL

Introduction

WHEN THE Committee for the Study of Incarceration first gathered in September 1971 to investigate the state of incarceration, it seemingly was acting in the best tradition of American reform. For as long as we have relied upon prisons and mental hospitals to treat and correct the deviant, so long have committees met to analyze the inadequacies of the institutions and to recommend improvements. In the nineteenth century, it was the task of the Philadelphia Society for Alleviating the Miseries of Public Prisons, the New York Prison Association, and the Boston Prison Discipline Society; in the twentieth, the work went to the Osborne Society and the National Committee for Mental Hygiene. Invariably, the results of such efforts were meager, at best promoting reform without change. And there was little reason to anticipate that anything very different would come from this group effort.

That our Committee was created and funded by foundations (the Field Foundation and the New World Foundation) concerned with the fate of the underprivileged in American society was also not unusual. In the 1930s, the Rockefeller Foundation supported a major reform effort to design and evaluate a model prison at Norfolk, Massachusetts. Nor did the fact that this Committee first met in the immediate aftermath of a prison crisis, Attica, represent a departure from custom. Prison riots typically have sparked a concern for institutional conditions. The late 1920s and early 1930s were, for example, a period of particular turmoil in prisons—and legislature after legislature established investigatory and study committees to report on the quality of prison life. That many members of the Committee came to this enterprise as critics of the incarceration system was not especially significant either. For at least a century, official and unofficial committees have begun their deliberations with a sharp sense of the failures of the institutions. They have all complained of antiquated facilities, massive overcrowding, the absence of vocational or rehabilitative programs, poor classification schemes, and untrained staff. There is nothing original in being a critic of American prisons or mental hospitals.

And yet, despite these continuities, this Committee effort has turned out to be a novel one, a departure from the usual ways of approaching incarceration. Unlike most of its predecessors, this Committee was prepared to address a first question: Ought we to have incarceration at all? Is it appropriate—for any purpose whatsoever—to place men or women behind walls, to resort to collective residential restraint? Practically every reform effort in our one-hundred-and-fifty-year history of incarceration has devoted the bulk of its energies to improving the state of the art, to designing programs that would ostensibly enhance the quality of institutional routines. Committees have typically accepted the propriety of incarceration, and then gone on to recommend the redesign of facilities, the better training of staff, the implementation of social service and educational programs. The charge of this committee was different—and the recommendations that emanate from it reflect this difference. Our question was whether this society ought *ever* to resort to incarceration, and if so, when, under what conditions, and for how long a period of time. The legitimacy of incarceration was thus the first item on our agenda.

The Committee, on its first day of meeting, shared another novel perspective: that incarceration was not a program exclusive to criminal justice. We recognized well that mental hospitals, juvenile reformatories, prisons, nursing homes, and boarding schools were more alike than they were different, in terms both of historical development and of the actualities of day-to-day routine. We hoped, too grandiosely it turned out, to address ourselves to the use of all these institutions, to answer the question of when it was appropriate to incarcerate *anyone*, whether that person came into the system through mental-health clinics, or criminal courts, or juvenile courts. We decided to tackle the toughest case first, where the right to incarcerate seemed presumptively most established; that is, the right of the state to incarcerate the criminal offender. Unfortunately, the Committee never did get beyond that issue. How marvelous it would have been to claim originality as a committee that actually fulfilled its agenda—but we cannot. Others will have to address the proprieties of incarceration in the fields of mental health and juvenile dependency and deviancy. We have here, for reasons of time and energy, limited ourselves to the test case of the adult, mentally competent offender.

THE METHODOLOGY of the Committee was at first as general as its original charge. Consistent with the fact that the majority of the members came from the social sciences and the law, we naturally adopted an approach that was essentially analytic. Reasonable and knowledgeable people, shaped in different disciplines and supported by differing fields of scholarship, would confront a problem together, pool their experiences and their judgment, and propose solutions. Our several heads would be better than one.

The group was interdisciplinary in the broadest sense; since the 1920s, sociologists and psychiatrists have evaluated institutional programs, and their presence on such a committee was logical. Lawyers were obviously also well represented, although, in truth, the legal profession has until recently played a lesser role in attempts to upgrade the system of incarceration. The Committee, of course, went beyond that. Philosopher, historian, economist, political scientist were each asked to join the effort. The group was a diverse one.

The group process, however, is not without difficulties. And interdisciplinary approaches have built-in hazards of their own. Imagine any one self-confident (if, hopefully, not arrogant) expert confronting a group in which each member may be as ignorant of his discipline as a freshman in an undergraduate class, but who brings to that assemblage not the humility of the uneducated but the authority and assurance of his own expertise. Imagine this group addressing the same problem but with different language, different premises, and indeed, often, a different style of reasoning, and some of the complexities become apparent.

Our goal was, in addition, not merely to produce a set of documents offering an economic, psychological, sociological, and legal solution to a problem (parallel thinking is not interdisciplinary), but rather to seek a unitary solution to a problem which would do justice to the purposes and intents, the perspectives and viewpoints of the various disciplines. In order to accomplish this, it is necessary for each expert to examine not just his vocabulary but the very premises of his profession—and to recognize that at the interface with other disciplines certain cherished values of one's profession may be irrelevant or harmful. At times it may even be necessary to sacrifice an ideal or a "truth" fundamental in one's professional practice, in order to serve the purposes of the group effort.

The psychoanalytically trained psychiatrist, for example, holds as one of his most fundamental tenets the concept of psychic determinism. He defines every individual act of behavior as the result of a multitude of emotional forces and counterforces built on past experience, so that all acts, healthy, sick, or not sure which, become predetermined. But determinism is antithetical to the social concept underlying criminal law, which must assume free will, or choice in action. It really is not important which concept is true, or if either is true. For certain purposes, either assumption may be useful or necessary; but to assume both at the same time is logically impossible. Obviously, if a psychiatrist is going to work within a system that requires personal responsibility, he must learn to draw distinctions from his experience about the nature of human beings and the nature of choice that are useful to those responsible for enforcement of law. He must find a way to accommodate his concept of psychic determinism with the free will necessary for assigning responsibility. This is but one of the dozens of essential contradictions that the members, by training, brought to the group.

However, there were factors in the structure of the group that facilitated communication—not the least of which was a general humility that most members felt in relation to this problem. All of us had individually worked with the problems of incarceration and had been frustrated and tormented by the lack of ready solutions. This disillusioning experience made us more ready for compromise than if we had all been new to the field.

Moreover, the Committee was bound by two overriding and unifying considerations: the sense of the injustices of the current system, and the need for a workable solution. There was always, therefore, a respect for the intentions of each fellow member, even when his articulations were mercilessly attacked.

In effect, then, this end product is a compromise—with all the limitations the word implies. It is unfortunate that a publication like this cannot be annotated (in the same way we annotate with scholarly references) with the recriminations, the cries of accusation, the sense of frustration, the internal tensions, the pleas, and the remorse that led to a final compromise position. Instead, the reader will encounter a bloodless statement about, for example, how much discretion the sentencing judge should have, without realizing the forces and counterforces that led to that seemingly simple and resultant notion. The language of compromise is never as romantic as evangelical furor, but in its way it involves as much passion, as much agony, and as much courage. Indeed, this introduction represents only the perspectives of a psychoanalyst and a historian who participated in what they found to be a stimulating venture.

THE PROBLEMS inherent in the subject of incarceration are formidable. Prisons are, after all, part of the broader institution of society—a criminal-justice system (which may explain why a committee established to study incarceration ends up publishing a book entitled *Doing Justice*, devoted mainly to the rationale of punishment). The purposes of that system have been particularly obscured by much of the current discussion, which tends to focus exclusively on the offender. But the system is, at its base, designed to serve not his needs but rather the needs of society.

Laws are established to maintain and preserve the social structure. In that sense, at least, the chief purpose of law is order, and the justice system is designed to serve the ends of the society at large. One of the sad consequences of the appropriation of the term "law and order" by the extreme right wing as a euphemism for racist feelings that were unfashionable to articulate was that the intellectual community, repelled by the implicit racism, turned away from the legitimate rights that such words imply. The authentic need to investigate the essential importance of both law and order was slighted. Instead, the intellectual community focused all too exclusively on the neglected rights of the criminal offender, forgetting that, while this was a compassionate and necessary pursuit, the welfare of the community was the primary concern of a system of criminal justice.

But if the primary purpose of law is order, it is not merely law *for* order. The orderly society is not necessarily the most desirable. A concentration camp is more orderly than a town meeting. Law, in a good society at least, must preserve not only the society but its ideals and values as well. And, in so doing, it must balance its desire for stability and order against its other values. Security, safety, survival may be fundamental—but there are limits. A good society must examine the methods of its survival to make sure that that which survives is still worthy. For that reason, one of the truest indices of the quality of life in a state is the way it responds to those who defy its laws.

The first question—to which this book devotes much attention—is to define the aims to be served in deciding how the law should respond to lawbreakers. Traditionally, five major aims are cited:

1. Restraint of the criminal. This, perhaps the simplest to understand, is often referred to as "prevention," or "incapacitation." When a person is confined, he is obviously unable to commit any crimes against the free members of society. He is incapacitated, and to the degree that he is unable to commit any crimes, the incidence of crime may go down. We may therefore be "preventing" a certain amount of crime from taking place.

2. General deterrence. If one person is punished for committing a crime, his publicized example might deter other would-be criminals from the same offense; this is the "frightening example," the dramatization of consequences.

3. Individual deterrence. If a person is punished for a crime, *he* might not be likely to repeat it. He might learn by experience.

4. Rehabilitation. During the last century and a half, this concept has dominated penal philosophy and rhetoric. It is part of a humanistic tradition which, in pressing for ever more individualization of justice, has demanded that we treat the criminal, not the crime. It relies upon a medical and educative model, defining the criminal as, if not sick, less than evil; somehow less "responsible" than he had previously been regarded. As a kind of social malfunctioner, the criminal needs to be "treated" or to be reeducated, reformed, or rehabilitated. Rehabilitation is, in many ways, the opposite of punishment. It pleads for a non-moral approach. At the same time, incarceration, as distinguished from more historic forms of punishment, allows the possibility, at least theoretically, of both punishment and education occurring simultaneously.

5. Desert. This idea has for some time been in disrepute, for many dismissed it as nothing but a polite term for vengeance. This book distinguishes between vengeance and desert, and shows that desert is a rich and important concept, grounded in ideas of fairness.

Whatever society's attitude toward the offender and his behavior, the punishment of the offender must incorporate the values that are respected and that define its concept of justice. But, like any other institution of the government, the methods it chooses will implicitly define the values of that government—and often more accurately than the explicit articulations of such values.

IT IS not difficult to understand or appreciate just how well the sanction of incarceration seemed to fit the values Americans believed fundamental to the administration of criminal justice. Americans, even in the twentieth century, still judged incarceration by looking backward to the sanctions it had replaced. From such an angle of vision, it seemed to represent a clear advance in humanitarianism. Our colonial forebears had relied upon far harsher measures to enforce order and justice. The lash had punished and deterred the petty offender; the gallows awaited the recidivist and those guilty of more serious crimes. We seemingly had abandoned retribution and such crude punishments. Indeed, reformers were generally reluctant to speculate on the demise of the penitentiary, fearing that the abolition of the prison would inevitably mean the return of the whip and gallows. Their view of the past, rather than liberating them to experiment with alternatives, committed them to defending the present.

In addition, beginning in the Progressive period and continuing until our own day, reformers saw incarceration as a marvelous opportunity to promote the welfare of the society along with the welfare of the offender. They could at once advance public safety and improve the lot of the criminal. This confidence reflected both a belief in the power of the system to effect rehabilitation and a trust in the discretion of the officials to know when to release or, conversely, how long to confine an offender.

In this context, the penitentiary was defined as a testing ground for society. The inmate who behaved himself behind the walls would conduct himself well in the community. And the prison would help him to perform well. Vocational programs would teach the skills and the habits necessary to hold a job; social-work counseling and elaborate classification schemes would move him stage by stage through the prison world; upon release, parole officers, as social workers, would assist him to integrate into the community. The offender would adjust to the society, not war with it. Of course, just as we did not tell doctors when to pronounce a patient cured, we were not, in the guise of fixed sentences, to tell wardens or parole boards when to release an inmate. The indeterminate sentence (from one day to life; or, less perfectly but still acceptably, from, say, two years to ten) was deemed essential to the proper working of the system. Each inmate was to be treated, like patients were treated, as an individual. In a country that prided itself on its individualism, it is hard to imagine a more appealing concept.

For its proponents, the system was elegant in that it benefited both the society and the offender. The rehabilitated offender was released to the community with skills and self-understanding that would guarantee his lawful behavior. Those who could not be rehabilitated—the chronically deviant, as it were—would be appropriately and properly kept in confinement for life, or at least for very long periods. Here was, then, a perfect way for society at once to do good and to protect itself.

Wardens, in this formulation, were experts—and one did not, as the courts did not, interfere with their conduct of the institutions. Small wonder, then, that the aftermath of each prison riot through the 1950s sparked well-meaning calls for building bigger prisons, for bringing in better staff, for upgrading the quality of prisons, not for abolishing them, or even curtailing their use.

This Committee began its deliberations suspicious of each

of these premises. The sanction of incarceration, we agreed, might prove worthy of preservation (in the end, as the reader will see, the Committee does not advocate its abolition), but our deliberations began without a prior commitment to this measure. Indeed, our deliberations opened without a commitment to any of the traditional rationales of punishment; rather, much of our effort was devoted to examining afresh the aims of punishment.

The roots of this skepticism differentiate us, as would-be reformers, from our predecessors. If Progressive reformers shared a basic trust in the state, more eager to involve its power in the society than to limit it, we as a group shared a basic mistrust of the power of the state. At the least we suspected that discretion might cloak discrimination and arbitrariness. We were certainly not prepared, a priori, to construct a system in which the benevolent motives of the administrators were sufficient reason to cloak them with power.

Moreover, we had good reason to be wary of the goal of rehabilitation. In our day-to-day experience, and in our preliminary research findings, it seemed that rehabilitation was far less often achieved than our predecessors would have believed. We could not, therefore, presuppose the validity or desirability of such a rationale. Further, we were not insensitive to the fact that a curious kind of shuffling between rehabilitation and incapacitation often went on within the institutions. Confront an administrator with the fact that his institution is not rehabilitating, and he would tell you he was confining dangerous people; tell him that not everyone inside the walls was dangerous, and he would respond that his was a therapeutic effort designed to rehabilitate the offender. The two goals seemed so in opposition to each other as to make us wary of just what social function the ethic of rehabilitation fulfilled.

Also, we were less prone than our predecessors to conceive of the offender as alien. Perhaps this was because the lawyers among us had defended black civil-rights agitators who entered jails and prisons in the early 1960s. Or perhaps because others among us had interviewed, counseled, and defended draft resisters to the Vietnam War in the 1960s. Or perhaps because some of us knew middle-class youngsters serving time for marijuana offenses. Or perhaps because several of us had visited prisons, had met prisoners, and could no longer think of them as a breed apart, somehow less human than the rest of us. In all events, we were prepared to start an inquiry with the assumption that prisoners had full rights, and then impose limits only where it seemed altogether necessary and appropriate.

Skepticism also breeds skepticism. Once it becomes the style of a committee, as it became the style of this one, to subject all premises to a simple but often devastating question—How do you know that? or, Why do you want that?—it turns out that, with regard to punishment in general and incarceration in particular, myth masquerades as fact and value choices frequently remain unexamined. Yes, deterrence has a common-sensical quality about it—but does it work? Does it work everywhere equally? Do you deter parking offenders as you deter murderers or armed bank robbers? And what of the equity in implementing deterrence? Are we ready to punish the one lawbreaker as an example to others? What of the offender's rights in this case? And how well does incapacitation serve us? What do we know of the system's ability to predict dangerousness? And what of the equities of incarcerating someone not for what he has done but for what he might do? In a moment we were at the basics of the case, forced to start our examination from the bottom up, to tackle first principles first, and see where all this led us. We might, we well realized, reinvent the wheel—but that was a risk we stood prepared to take.

BOTH IN tone and in content, the recommendations of the Committee represent a departure from tradition. Permeating this report is a determination to do less rather than more—an insistence on not doing harm. The quality of heady optimism and confidence of reformers in the past, and their belief that they could solve the problem of crime and eradicate the presence of deviancy, will not be found in this document. Instead, we have here a crucial shift in perspective from a commitment to do good to a commitment to do as little mischief as possible.

One may well be nostalgic for a time when reformers could parade under a banner of progress, claiming to have at hand the cure for social evils. But that nostalgia, however acutely felt, ought not to shape public policy. Not only because past reforms all too regularly bred the most undesirable results (the rise of the asylum producing, finally, warehouses for people), but because we are now forced to confront, as our predecessors were not, our own inabilities to understand the roots of crime and deviancy or to fashion programs that effect good. Thus, however modest these new proposals, they are intended to generate less disastrous consequences than the programs we now administer.

The Committee has attempted to translate this sense of restraint into a series of proposals that look to limiting state intervention, to reducing discretion, and to scaling down the levels of punishment. It proposes a series of "warnings" for crimes low on a scale of seriousness, intermittent confinement (weekends or evenings) for more serious offenses, and permits full-time incarceration only for the most serious crimes. Even in that category, it insists that the state do less and not more; that it scale down the length of sentences to the point where it satisfies our sense of equity, but no more than that. The Committee insists that the potential benefit done to any one offender under a system of massive discretion is more than offset by the harms done to the vast majority of persons through such a normless scheme, and hence advocates the abolition of the indeterminate sentence and the adoption of sentencing standards that limit judicial discretion.

In this same spirit, the Committee has not called for abolition, immediate or gradual, of all incarceration. This unwillingness to stand for abolition despite our acute awareness of the inhumanity of present conditions, our sense of the inability of courts or administrative agencies to effect meaningful change in the quality of prison life, and the strongly felt desire on the part of at least some members of the Committee to be done with this horrendous system once and for all, reflect several important considerations. For one, we are not persuaded that any program currently in vogue or under discussion for the serious offender—and it is exclusively this group that we are prepared to incarcerate —seems any less mischievous than the prison. Prisons, at least, have confined the despotism of the state behind walls. Behavior modification, electrode implantation, tracking devices could bring despotism into every community. We must not deinstitutionalize offenders at the price of institutionalizing the rest of us.

For another, the Committee was prepared to accept a model based essentially on judgments about equity and commensurate deserts, to elevate primarily moral judgments in the field of criminal justice, because it firmly believed that the limitations thereby imposed on the state more than outweighed considerations that justice could never be served in a society dominated by inequities and inequalities. Not that many of us on the Committee do not appreciate just how uneven the distribution of power, property, and rights is in this society. Not that many of us do not foresee the need for a fundamental redistribution of power and property to fulfill the claim that ours is a just society. Rather, we contend that the ultimate and critical value in a concept like desert rests in its ability to preserve and promote decent and accepted values in this society and at the same time to restrain the state from infringing on individual rights in the administration of criminal justice.

THE RETENTION of incarceration was not a conclusion necessarily anticipated of, or by, this Committee. We are aware that some of the conclusions offered may seem inconsistent with previous recommendations and positions of the individual members of the group and may surprise many readers. If the explicit practices of a group define its real values, as distinguished from its articulated code of ethics, which merely defines its aspirations, then what of this Committee and its recommendations? What can we say of a group which, when faced with the choice of rehabilitation or desert, opts for desert?

It is not easy to abandon the rehabilitative model, for it was a scheme born to optimism, and faith, and humanism. It viewed the evils in man as essentially correctable, and only partially the responsibility of the individual. The ultimate exponent of the view is probably Dr. Karl Menninger, and it is not just coincidence that he is a psychiatrist. The very title of his most recent book, *The Crime of Punishment*, indicated his feeling that a psychiatric model was the only appropriate one for criminal offenders. Perhaps more than any other, he took us closer to the brave new world of Aldous Huxley, in which the announcement that someone had committed a crime elicited the compassionate response, "I did not know he was ill." This approach was always under attack from the conservative community, to which it had appeared as a mollycoddling, bleeding-heart outrage, and now we find ourselves, for different reasons, with different motives, joining the argument for its abandonment. We believe the rehabilitative model abounded with internal inconsistencies which inevitably offered opportunities for exploitation—that were, just as inevitably, accepted. It produced unexpected abhorrent consequences and numerous unpredicted side effects that were less humane or liberal than its proponents had anticipated.

When one switches from a frame of reference which is judgmental and punitive to one that is medical, a whole range of corollaries are brought into play. Part of the inherent definition of a sick person is a presumption of non-culpability for his disease; when we say "It's not his fault, he is sick," we are defining the patient as the victim, not the victimizer. This was an especially attractive premise for the humane and optimistic legal philosophers.

But the therapeutic model is a complicated one. To some

members of the Committee, it still may hold the highest
ideal, and they abandon it with great reluctance. Crucial
practical and moral difficulties are encountered, however,
when this ideal is incorporated into the compulsory processes of the criminal law. The simple fact is that the
experiment has not worked out. Despite every effort and
every attempt, correctional treatment programs have failed.
The supporters of rehabilitation will say, and perhaps
rightly so, that it was never really given a complete chance,
that it was only accepted in theory while in practice the
system has insisted on maintaining punitive practices. On
the other hand, the question remains whether one can
reasonably continue to expect anything different, given the
extended trial that rehabilitation has had.

Moreover, the rehabilitative model, despite its emphasis
on understanding and concern, has been more cruel and
punitive than a frankly punitive model would probably be.
Medicine is allowed to be bitter; inflicted pain is not
cruelty, if it is treatment rather than punishment. Under the
rehabilitative model, we have been able to abuse our
charges, the prisoners, without disabusing our consciences.
Beneath this cloak of benevolence, hypocrisy has flourished,
and each new exploitation of the prisoner has inevitably
been introduced as an act of grace. Finally, to sentence
people guilty of similar crimes to different dispositions in
the name of rehabilitation—to punish not for act but for
condition—violates, this book argues, fundamental concepts
of equity and fairness. And so we as a group, trained in
humanistic traditions, have ironically embraced the seemingly harsh principle of just deserts.

When punishment is expressed in these terms, it abandons its primary reliance upon a utilitarian rationale. As

such, it is justified not as an effective crime-prevention measure but because it is right—because it ought to be. There is the feeling of a Kantian imperative behind the word "deserts." Certain things are simply wrong and ought to be punished. And this we do believe.

In so stating our position, we then become free to set reasonable limits to the extent of punishment. When we honestly face the fact that our purpose is retributive, we may, with a re-found compassion and a renewed humanity, limit the degree of retribution we will exact.

And still we are not happy. Our solution is one of despair, not hope. We recognize that, in giving up the rehabilitative model, we abandon not just our innocence but perhaps more. The concept of deserts is intellectual and moralistic; in its devotion to principle, it turns back on such compromising considerations as generosity and charity, compassion and love. It emphasizes justice, not mercy, and while it need not rule out tempering justice with mercy, by shifting the emphasis from concern for the individual to devotion to the moral right, it could lead to an abandonment of the former altogether. We also recognize that, while rehabilitation may have been used as an excuse for heaping punishment upon punishment, it also was a limiting factor, and was a rationalization and justification for what few comforts were introduced into the lives of the prisoners.

What we offer are partial solutions, while awaiting more insights, greater knowledge, and more complete answers in some hoped-for future. And central to our conception, essential to its balance, is a commitment to the most stringent limits on incarceration.

It would be better to ignore the recommendations of the Committee entirely than to accept any part of them without that focus on decarceration about which all its other arguments pivot. It is crucial that mandated sentences should range, in most cases, closer to the current minimum than to the current maximum. This is not simply out of compassion for the prisoner—although compassion is a scarce commodity in his world—but as a matter of justice and common sense. Prisons may not be criminogenic institutions, but they are certainly not crime-curing. They are wasteful, expensive, and ultimately destructive of our self-respect. The public must understand this so as to become less vulnerable to the cant and rhetoric of elected public officials who cover every conceivable ineptitude and inadequacy on their part with a call for more lockups. To abandon the rehabilitative model without a simultaneous gradation downward in prison sentences would be an unthinkable cruelty and a dangerous act.

Perhaps it is not the most compelling advertisement for one's committee to conclude that the principles we advocate here will do less mischief and perpetuate less inequity than the system with which we now live. But if we can deflate the rhetoric and limit the reach of programs that now pretend to do good, then our time and energy has been well spent. We believe that we offer a model which holds promise of workability. And still we know that even if all that we recommend is effected, we have an imperfect system.

We recognize that by retreating from a concept of individualized justice, discretion in sentencing, we are giving up an important aspiration. But such a shift, forced by our own limitations, our narrowness, our meanness, our sense of the other as alien and the alien as enemy, each abandonment of an ideal, will exact a cost. We are recommending a greater mechanization of justice because we have not achieved either the individual love and understanding or the social distribution of power and property that is essential if discretion is to serve justice.

We are not so naïve as not to recognize that we will pay a price. Each retreat from individualism in one field will extend to others, ultimately diminishing the position of every individual. It matters little whether the field is criminal justice or the practice of medicine. More and more, in the push for space, food, and pleasures, we are progressively being reduced and regimented, homogenized and dehumanized. In abandoning individualism here, we make it progressively easier to abandon it elsewhere. Perhaps we can anticipate a time when with new insights, and new institutions, a different group of individuals in a different social setting will reconvene and once again discover the amoral, non-judgmental world of the rehabilitative model.

WILLARD GAYLIN
DAVID J. ROTHMAN

Doing Justice
The Choice of Punishments

1

Dimensions of the Study

WHAT SHOULD be done with the criminal offender after conviction?

The need for a theoretical framework to answer this question has been made apparent by recent disclosures about prisons. While prisons have been the mainstay of America's correctional system since the 1820s,[1] their walls hid much of the painfulness of life inside. In the last three decades, however, prisons and other places of confinement have been subjected to closer scrutiny. Sociologists and psychologists documented their social life;[2] courts inquired into institutional conditions;[3] inmates made their grievances heard.[4] Incarceration, it became apparent, is a far harsher measure than was once supposed.

These disclosures compel a reassessment of the prison sanction. Is it really necessary to inflict so much suffering?

Might not less painful penalties serve the aims of criminal justice as well? Not surprisingly, there has been much recent interest in drastically reducing the use of prisons, and developing alternatives to incarceration. Yet the search for alternatives has been complicated by a new uncertainty about goals.

Twenty years ago, the aim seemed clear: to rehabilitate the offender. Treatment programs were being implemented as never before. But researchers were disappointed when they began monitoring the programs: most methods of treatment (both inside prisons and in the community) were found not to work.[5] It also became apparent that the ideal of treatment was not without its own dangers: it legitimized *more* state intervention with fewer legal and moral constraints.[6]

Such doubts complicate the search for alternatives to imprisonment. Looking for better ways of treating offenders does not suffice: for it is no longer clear that rehabilitation can realistically be (or even should be) the aim. A fundamental reexamination of goals has become necessary.

This book undertakes such a reexamination. We shall try to develop a rationale for the disposition of convicted criminals. Our purpose is to identify the principles that should govern decisions about how severely offenders should be punished. Using such principles, we shall suggest when, if ever, incarceration should be used as punishment; and how non-incarcerative penalties can be developed and employed.

We will be concerned only with convicted adults, not with more complex questions presented by juvenile offenders. What constitutes adulthood is itself debatable—but, for our purposes, persons of eighteen or over are deemed adults, for at that age they have most adult prerogatives: to live independent of parental supervision, own and manage property, vote, and be free of "beneficial" state compulsion such as required school attendance. We will be concerned with the adult offender at the "dispositional" stage of the criminal process—the stage following the finding or plea of guilt, when the decision is made how he should be punished. Our analysis will rest on certain moral premises.

The liberty of each individual, we assume, is to be protected so long as it is consistent with the liberty of others.

We assume also that the state is obligated to observe strict parsimony in intervening in convicted offenders' lives.[7] Even after conviction, the state should have the burden of justifying why any given degree of intrusion—and not a lesser one—is called for. Severe penalties should bear an especially heavy burden of justification.

Finally, we assume that the requirements of *justice* ought to constrain the pursuit of crime prevention. That assumption represents a departure from tradition. It was commonly supposed that justice had largely been satisfied once an offender was tried and convicted with due process. Thereafter, attention turned almost exclusively to crime prevention: penologists were preoccupied with which theories (rehabilitation, incapacitation, or deterrence) or which tactics (more severity or less) promoted public safety best. Seldom was the word "justice" even mentioned in the literature of sentencing and corrections.

While people will disagree about what justice requires, our assumption of the primacy of justice is vital because it alters the terms of the debate. One cannot, on this assumption, defend any scheme for dealing with convicted criminals solely by pointing to its usefulness in controlling crime: one is compelled to inquire whether that scheme is a just one and why.

This book is conceptual, setting forth principles, not a program for enactment. Our aim is to provide a structure of ideas, against which specific programs may be judged. We deliberately disregard the politics of reform—whether a suggested improvement is likely (or unlikely) to be implemented at present. We are aware that reformers, pursuing the practical business of change, have to accommodate their aims to political and institutional realities. But a wise accommodation requires, first, a coherent conception: without an idea of what a rational and fair system might be, it is difficult to decide which compromises to make to achieve even a partially adequate system.

Ours is also, deliberately, an argumentative book. In setting forth our case as strongly as we can, we have omitted much of the flavor of the Committee's own discussions—the tensions of opposing arguments and the doubts we felt along the way. We hope our systematic, argumentative approach will present a thesis plainly: that it will stimulate questions and criticisms.

Some of our conclusions may seem old-fashioned. To our surprise, we found ourselves returning to the ideas of such Enlightenment thinkers as Kant and Beccaria—ideas that antedated notions of rehabilitation that emerged in the nineteenth century. We take seriously Kant's view that a person should be punished because he deserves it. We argue, as both Kant and Beccaria did, that severity of punishment should depend chiefly on the seriousness of the crime. We share Beccaria's interest in placing limits on sentencing discretion. If returning to these conceptions seems a step into the past, it may be some consolation that the ideas underlying the Bill of Rights are no younger.

I

The Conventional Assumptions

"PERSONS CONVICTED of crime shall be dealt with in accordance with their potential for rehabilitation, considering their individual characteristics, circumstances and needs. . . . [D]angerous offenders shall be identified, segregated, and correctively treated in custody for as long terms as needed." [1] This quotation is from the 1972 edition of the Model Sentencing Act, an influential piece of model legislation prepared under the auspices of the National Council on Crime and Delinquency. It is a succinct restatement of conventional assumptions that, for nearly a century, have dominated thinking about the disposition of convicted offenders.

The conventional viewpoint consists of three main assumptions.

The first and most prominent has been that the disposition should rehabilitate: the offender should receive the correctional treatment best suited to inculcate law-abiding habits in him. Rehabilitation should influence the choice of sentence as well as the manner in which the sentence is carried out.

Predictive restraint is a second theme. The disposition, supposedly, should be based on a forecast of the offender's likelihood of returning to crime. If he is considered a potential recidivist, he should be confined until he becomes safe.

Individualized decision-making is the third. The disposition is to be tailored to the offender's need for treatment and the risk he poses to the public. To allow decisions to be individualized, sentencing courts and correctional officials are to be given wide discretionary powers of disposition, with as few legal constraints as possible.

During the first half of this century, these ideas had almost unchallenged ascendancy. While less fashionable notions (such as deterrence and desert) did retain a measure of influence on the practical decisions of legislatures and judges, the dominant trio of assumptions was thought to represent the enlightened viewpoint. In the last two decades, skepticism about these notions has been growing, but the conventional assumptions retain considerable influence. In crime commission reports, judicial opinions, and editorials, the familiar themes are still reiterated: sentence for treatment, incarcerate the dangerous, individualize the disposition.[2] We thus think it necessary to sketch some of the deficiencies of the conventional assumptions before developing our own theory.

2

The Rehabilitative Disposition

REHABILITATION,* according to the conventional assumptions, is the preeminent goal. The sentence itself is seen as an instrument for treatment: when deciding between imprisonment and probation, for example, the sentencer is supposed to take into account which disposition will best

---

* We define "rehabilitation" as any measure taken to change an offender's character, habits, or behavior patterns so as to diminish his criminal propensities. Rehabilitation, then, is a particular mode of crime control—one that seeks to alter the offender so he is less inclined to offend again. In the literature of rehabilitation, there is often considerable ambiguity whether the aim is to reduce recidivism (a form of crime prevention) or to help the offender with his own problems (a paternalistic goal). But treatment programs have generally been tested by measuring their effects on recidivism—suggesting that the goal of reducing recidivism is actually the primary one.

Rehabilitation, by our definition, includes not only traditional treatments (psychiatric therapy, counseling, vocational training, etc.) but also more novel methods of curbing recidivism such as behavior-modification techniques.

promote the offender's rehabilitation. Thus, the American Law Institute's Model Penal Code, completed in 1962, recommends that a sentencing court may choose prison rather than probation if, among other reasons, the offender is "in need of correctional treatment that can be provided most effectively by his commitment to an institution." ° [1]

Since this theory looks to offenders' need for treatment rather than to the character of their crimes, it allows different sentences for similar offenses. If one of two convicted burglars is thought likely to respond to community-based treatment while the other seems more amenable to a prison-based program, that would be reason for putting one on probation and imprisoning the other. The difference in the two sentences is rationalized as necessary for the protection of the public: the two burglars will be less likely to return to crime if each is given treatment suited to his particular need. That explanation holds, however, only if the programs work. Unless the programs can demonstrably prevent recidivism, the discrepancy in the two dispositions remains unaccounted for. It is therefore essential to ask: How effective are treatment programs? † [2]

° The Model Penal Code's recommendation is reiterated in subsequent commission reports—namely, in the American Bar Association's proposed standards for sentencing; in the federal criminal code proposed in 1971 by the National Advisory Commission on Reform of Federal Criminal Laws; and, most recently (in 1973), in the report of the National Advisory Commission on Criminal Justice Standards and Goals.

† Effectiveness is distinct from another issue that has stirred much debate: the influence of the ideal of treatment on penal practice. Rehabilitatively oriented reformers claim that the goal of rehabilitation has been a civilizing influence in the correctional system. Critics argue that the treatment ideology has done just the opposite: to impart a misleading impression of beneficence to the harsh realities of punishing people, and to legitimize more intervention in offenders' lives with fewer constraints on official behavior. (This criticism was first stated by the former

Proponents of correctional treatment once had reason to complain that their methods had never really been given a chance to work. Prison administrators, while long on talk about rehabilitation, were short on programs: the available "treatments" did little more than train convicts in skills for which there existed no market in the outside world, such as making license plates. But during recent decades—especially in California—seriously thought-out and well-financed experimental programs have been tried. The results have not been encouraging.

Ask a warden or prison psychologist why his favorite rehabilitation program is effective, and he may tell you he has seen it work: former incorrigibles who participated now keep out of trouble. But that "proof" is illusory: for the "cured" individuals might have stopped offending without any program—because of advancing age, diminishing criminal opportunities, or whatever. To judge the effectiveness of a program, one must evaluate it comparatively: how much better do offenders placed in the program perform than those with similar characteristics who did not participate? No program is proven effective unless those enrolled in it show a consistently lower rate of return to crime than comparable offenders not enrolled.* 3

dean of the University of Michigan Law School, Francis Allen, in a collection of essays published in 1964 entitled *The Borderland of Criminal Justice.* For a further elaboration, we refer the reader to the American Friends' Service Committee's fine book, *Struggle for Justice* [1971]; and to an article by David Rothman in the Fall 1973 issue of the *Civil Liberties Review* entitled "Decarcerating Prisoners and Patients.")

* The critical question is whether the enrolled and non-enrolled groups are, in fact, comparable. If they are not, the measure of effectiveness is misleading. One instance is the widely publicized "positive" outcome of the Manhattan Court Employment Project, a pretrial diversion program in which defendants were referred for group therapy and employment counseling. A subsequent analysis of the data by Franklin Zimring of the University of Chicago Law School disclosed

A wide variety of rehabilitation programs have now been studied. A few successes have been reported, but the overall results are disappointing.[4] Thus, for example:

• The character of the institution seems to have little or no influence on recidivism. It was hoped that prisoners in smaller and less regimented institutions would return to crime less often on release, but that hope has not been borne out.[5]

• Although probation has long been acclaimed for its rehabilitative usefulness, the recidivism rate among otherwise like offenders fails to show a clear difference whether they are placed on probation or confined. While those on probation perform no worse, the claim that they perform better has not been sustained.[6]

• More intensive supervision on the streets, a recurring theme in rehabilitation literature, has not been shown to curb recidivism. Probationers or parolees assigned to small caseloads with intense supervision appear to return to crime about as often as those assigned to large caseloads with minimal supervision.[7]

• Vocational training has been widely advocated, on the

---

that the experimental group was more carefully screened (and thus possibly contained lower risks) than the control group—thus rendering the results suspect.

Another problem is the reliability of the recidivism statistics. Usually, researchers measure the rate of return to crime by some kind of official response to criminal behavior—arrests, convictions, parole revocations, or the like. That can be a source of error, as the official response may have built-in biases. A striking instance was a California study that claimed effectiveness for an experimental program of small-caseload probation. The figures showed that those enrolled in the program had a lower incidence of probation revocations than probationers assigned to regular caseloads. But later it was found that probation officers were so enthusiastic about use of small caseloads that they were more lenient in dealing with probation violations by individuals enrolled in that program than with violations by those on regular probation. That, of course, vitiated the findings.

theory that people turn to crime because they lack the skills
enabling them to earn a lawful living. The quality of many
programs has been poor. But where well-staffed and
well-equipped programs of vocational training for marketable skills have been tried in institutions, studies fail to show
a lower rate of return to crime.[8] In California, where this
technique has most extensively been used, authorities have
all but given up hope. A 1971 official evaluation of
vocational training concludes: "Profiting from the experience of history, the Department of Corrections does not
claim that vocational training has any particular capability
of reducing recidivism." [9] Nor has education and literacy
training[10]—or psychiatrically oriented counseling programs[11]
—had appreciably greater success.

  • In the late 1960s, "community-based" treatment received increased emphasis. It was thought that offenders'
chances for being rehabilitated would be enhanced if the
treatment were undertaken in their home neighborhoods.
Some of these "community-based" programs consisted of
intensive counseling or other therapy conducted in small,
residential facilities located in low-income neighborhoods;
others consisted of daytime treatment programs that allowed the participants to live at home. Results thus far have
not been encouraging.[12] (Some proponents of community
treatment have tried to turn the disappointing results to
their advantage. While the community programs generally
did no better than prison-based methods, they also did no
worse: the former thus are preferable, it is argued, because
they are more humane and less costly.[13] This argument,
however, overshoots its mark: what the evidence indicates
could simply be the failure of treatment—so that the same

results might have been attained without *any* treatment.)° [14]

Some advocates of rehabilitation attribute the current failures to inadequate screening. Programs are applied indiscriminately to heterogeneous groups of offenders, some of whom may be responsive while others are not. The successes might be canceled out by the failures—because so many of the participants were unsuited to the approach used. It is, they say, like using insulin to treat all diseases: diabetics who improved would have to be counted against non-diabetics who died of insulin shock, leaving the overall cure rate little different than that for untreated patients. Arguably, outcomes could begin to improve were one able, in rehabilitation as in medicine, to identify with greater precision the particular subgroups of offenders who are amenable to different types of treatment.[15] However, ignorance of the causes of crime remains a serious barrier to successful screening.† [16]

° There have, for instance, been several much-publicized programs that place juvenile offenders in "open" residential facilities or day programs, where control is less overtly authoritarian, and where group counseling or other forms of psychological therapy are important parts of the routine. Attempts are made to enlist peer pressure in support of law-abiding behavior and values, and prevent the formation of an inmate "code" hostile to the staff. Serious methodological flaws mar the evaluations of most of these studies, but universally, they report that boys sent to such programs perform no worse—although not consistently any better— after release than those sent to reformatories. Proponents argue that such programs are therefore preferable to reformatories, since they are cheaper and less brutalizing and yet produce no more recidivism. But few, if any, studies have attempted to compare the outcome of these community programs with that of matched samples of youth placed on conventional probation (or outright release) without therapy. The latter measures would, of course, be still less costly to operate (and involve less intrusion into the offender's life). If the rate of return to crime were no higher, why the therapy at all?

† Insulin can be prescribed for diabetes but not for other conditions, because diabetes has been successfully identified as a disease related to insulin deficiency.

Behavior control is another technique that has recently been tried. ("If Freud can't cure criminals, why not try Skinner?") Such methods (including aversive conditioning, chemotherapy, and psychosurgery) have been used primarily in mental hospitals, but occasionally some have been tried in prisons.[17] While there have been claims for their effectiveness in controlling disruptive behavior within the institution,[18] their long-term rehabilitative usefulness has yet to be demonstrated.* [19] And where sufficiently painful, debilitating, or intrusive, these techniques deserve to be ruled out on ethical grounds irrespective of effectiveness.†

When doctors are ignorant of the origins of a condition, their capacity for cure diminishes. But, in the field of crime, ignorance of causes is the rule. Even without an etiology of various kinds of criminal behavior, one could resort to elimination by trial and error. One could, for example, begin with a large heterogeneous sample and treat that sample. Subgroups that are the least responsive would be dropped, as would aspects of the treatment that show the poorest results. By successively narrowing the sample and revising the treatment technique, one might arrive at a subgroup for whom a particular technique shows a better outcome. However, this is not only a slow process—but a cumbersome one, since numerous variables have to be compared. One study of group counseling considered thirty offender and treatment variables—but still was not able to find significant relationships (and the mathematical complexities were staggering). If the key to effective rehabilitation lies in better screening, the road to success may be a long one.

* As Harvard psychologist Ralph Schwitzgebel notes of aversive conditioning methods: ". . . unless the stimuli are very intense, aversive suppression generally does not completely eliminate the occurrence of the punished behavior but rather lowers its rate, which may gradually, without additional suppression, return to its approximate pre-punishment rate. There are also occasional 'paradoxical' effects of punishment in which the use of aversive stimuli may increase the rate of the punished behavior when the aversive stimuli are removed. [And] punishment may produce side effects such as anxiety or deception which ultimately make the behavior increase."

† For a discussion of the ethical issues of behavior control as applied to offenders, see, e.g., Vernon H. Mark and Robert Neville, "Brain Surgery in Aggressive Epileptics," 226 *J. Amer. Medical Ass'n* 765 (1973); Michael H. Shapiro, "Legislating the Control of Behavior Control: Autonomy and the Coercive Use of Organic Therapies," 47 *S. Cal. L. Rev.* 237 (1974).

It would be an exaggeration to say that no treatment methods work, for some positive results have been reported, which further follow-up may confirm. But, certainly, few programs seem to succeed; and it is still uncertain to what extent the claimed successes would survive replication or closer analysis.

In those special instances where it might be possible to find treatment that works, the more difficult question has to be confronted: Aside from effectiveness, what other limitations should there be on the rehabilitative disposition? Is it just, for example, to impose dissimilar sentences for treatment purposes upon offenders convicted of similar crimes? We shall argue later that there are limitations of justice on the rehabilitative disposition, even if the treatment were known to be effective.

But in the more commonplace instances where no successful treatments are known, the rehabilitative disposition is plainly untenable. It cannot be rational or fair to sentence for treatment, without a reasonable expectation that the treatment works.

3

Predictive Restraint

RESTRAINT OF the potential recidivist—"predictive restraint," as we shall call it—is the second of the conventional assumptions. If the offender is thought likely to offend again, he should be incapacitated so that he cannot do so.* The idea has been endorsed by the Model Penal Code, which states that an offender may be confined if the sentencing judge finds ". . . there is undue risk that during the period of a suspended sentence or probation the defendant will commit another crime." †¹ The Model

---

* Predictive restraint is a narrower concept than incapacitation, in that the selection of *which* individuals are to be incapacitated is made on the basis of a prediction of their criminal tendencies. It is the predictive criterion of selection that presents problems of fairness, as we discuss in this chapter. The idea of incapacitation may have more merit were it employed with a different (and fairer) criterion of selection—a possibility we consider in Chapter 13.

† This general authority for predictive restraint is in addition to the Model Penal Code's provisions for extended prison terms for specific classes of offenders deemed especially dangerous.

Sentencing Act° [2] relies still more heavily on prediction of future criminality in deciding which convicted offenders are to be confined. (Predictive restraint is also very much part of today's sentencing practice. It is routine for sentencing judges and parole boards to try to gauge whether the convicted defendant is apt to revert to his criminal ways. If he is considered a potential recidivist, he is more likely to go to prison and stay there longer.)[3]

Historically, the idea of predictive restraint was linked to rehabilitation: the offender was to be treated—but, if likely to offend again, would be isolated from the community while receiving treatment.[4] Recently, however, the notion is coming to stand on its own. Even if the capacity for cure is lacking, it is argued, the public can be protected by identifying potential recidivists and holding them as long as they are likely to commit further crimes.[5] The idea of simple restraint is substituted for therapy.

Restraining persons thought likely to return to crime seems sensible enough: whatever other disadvantages incarceration may have, it can prevent criminally inclined individuals from offending against persons outside—at least during their confinement. If incarceration serves this purpose, what more logical way is there of selecting which offenders are to be confined, and for how long, than by assessing their criminal propensities? But this assumes that one can, indeed, forecast recidivism accurately; and, not surprisingly, the proponents of preventive intervention claim much predictive acuity. The drafters of the Model

---

° In its 1972 edition, the Act asserts that the principal ground for confining an offender is that he is dangerous—whereas, in the Model Penal Code, likelihood of returning to crime is listed as one of three grounds for confinement.

Sentencing Act, for example, assert that the Act's "definition of 'dangerous offenders' together with the procedure for referral for clinical diagnosis makes it possible for the first time to achieve reasonable accuracy in identifying such persons." [6]

But the ability to predict dangerousness has not lived up to such hopes. One reason for error has been that predicters—be they judges, psychiatrists, or correctional officials—seldom have taken the trouble to follow up their forecasts and check their accuracy, and thus learn from their mistakes.[7] But even were forecasts verified systematically, that still would not yield the "reasonable accuracy" of which the Model Sentencing Act speaks so optimistically. For a more fundamental problem is encountered: an inherent tendency to overpredict.

The forecasting of criminal behavior has been a topic of interest to criminologists for nearly half a century—since E. W. Burgess at the University of Chicago published the first prediction table for parole recidivism in 1928.[8] But as Leslie Wilkins has noted,[9] the forecasters' criterion of accuracy has tended to be one-sided—looking only to success in identifying those persons who subsequently *do* offend. Overprediction, the other side of the coin, is seldom considered: in how many instances does the prediction yield what statisticians call "false positives"—persons mistakenly predicted to offend? When forecasting assaultive behavior, for example, how many individuals predicted to commit assaults would have turned out subsequently *not* to attack anyone? When prediction is being relied upon to determine whether and for how long a convicted offender is to be confined, mistakenly classifying him as a potential recidivist has the gravest consequences—the extended loss of his liberty.°

The tendency to overpredict derives from the comparative rarity of the conduct to be predicted. Serious crimes are, statistically speaking, infrequent events; and the rarer the event, the greater will be the incidence of false positives. Thus:

• Methods of predicting criminal behavior, whether clinical or statistical, are blunt instruments. Unlike the incipient tubercular, the potential recidivist does not carry easily spotted symptoms of his condition; the predicter has to rely on correlations between offenders' currently observed characteristics and any subsequent criminal behavior on their part. The data will necessarily be crude: only grossly observable characteristics of the offender population can ordinarily be identified; and the measurement of outcome—subsequent criminal conduct—is notoriously unreliable, given the problems of undetected violations and selective enforcement.

• If the conduct to be predicted occurs rarely in the sample, the crudity of these inputs takes its toll. With a predictive instrument of so little discernment and a target population so small, the forecaster will be able to spot a significant percentage of the actual violators *only if a large number of false positives is also included.* The process resembles trying to hit a small bull's-eye with a blunderbuss: to strike the center of the target with any of the shot, the marksman will have to allow most of his discharge to hit outside it.† [10]

° The offender's confinement might have to be lengthy, if the aim is to prevent the offender from offending again. He would have to be held until his predicted criminal tendencies abated—which might take years, especially if there is no effective treatment that could be administered during confinement.

† These difficulties in predicting infrequent behavior were pointed out in an illuminating article written more than twenty years ago by the psychologist Albert

This has been confirmed in a 1971 study of violent crimes by the criminologists Ernst Wenk, James Robison, and Robert Emrich.[11] Their study concerned a group of youthful offenders who had been committed to the California Youth Authority. Since nearly one quarter of the youths in the sample had a history of violent behavior, the potential in this group for new violence was expected to be high. Their behavior on parole was followed up for a period of fifteen months after their release from confinement, with a view to determining how many were returned for assaultive offenses. The investigators found that the incidence of violent recidivism during the fifteen-month follow-up period was only 2.4 percent.* A rate that low could be expected to yield a large number of false positives—and that is precisely what happened. The investigators requested a psychologist and a statistician to develop predictive indices for violent recidivism, based upon the data in their sample. The less

---

Rosen of the University of Minnesota. Rosen took as his example the prediction of suicide in mental hospitals. Suicide is statistically rare. It is rare (or at least Rosen assumed it to be so, on the basis of the data then available) even among mental patients. He assumed the incidence of suicide in a mental hospital (the "base rate" in statisticians' jargon) to be about one third of one percent; so that in a large hospital of 12,000 patients, there would be 40 actual suicides. Rosen then postulated a hypothetical predictive index capable of successfully identifying 75 percent of the suicidal and 75 percent of the non-suicidal patients—a much better performance than the available predictive indices were, in fact, capable of. This hypothetical index could successfully identify a substantial majority—thirty out of forty—of the actual suicides. But it did so at the cost of misidentifying nearly 3,000 non-suicidal patients as suicidal. When a higher proportion (99.5 percent) of the non-suicidal patients was screened out, the number of false positives dropped to 60. But then, the index succeeded in spotting only one out of forty actual suicides.

* The 2.4% rate represents the rate of *known* violent recidivist offenses among this group. Because of undetected crimes, the actual rate may well have been substantially higher: but even assuming that the rate of violent recidivism is three or four times as much, that still would not be sufficient to avoid the false-positive problem here described.

pessimistic projection—the psychologist's—was that a predictive instrument could be developed from the data which could identify about one half of the true positives—but in which the false positives outnumbered the true by a discouraging eight to one.* [12]

There will be fewer false positives if less serious infractions are taken into account—for these are not so rare. Even a crude forecasting instrument will not overpredict much if the event to be predicted occurs frequently in the sample.[13] (It is like our marksman with the blunderbuss aiming at a very large target.) In the sample used in the Wenk-Robison-Emrich study,[14] the recidivism rate rises to a more manageable 40 percent when not only violent crimes but other parole violations are included. But to obtain this higher rate, one finds oneself fast descending the scale of seriousness toward lesser violations. As that happens, it becomes increasingly difficult to demonstrate a need for protecting society that is of sufficient urgency to warrant the deprivation of the offender's freedom.†

Overprediction has disturbing implications. It suggests not merely that the predictions are fallible (what judgments are not?) but that they are prone to be grossly in error: most of those deemed to be risks—and confined on that account —may have been misclassified. Whatever the utility of holding those offenders who would in fact offend again,

---

* More recently, Harry Kozol and his associates attempted to predict assaultive behavior among a group of individuals more than half of whom had a prior history of serious assaultive conduct. Even among this high-risk sample, however, the false positives substantially outnumbered the true.

† For a discussion of this point—the relationship between the seriousness of the harm to be prevented and the extent of predictive intervention—see Alan M. Dershowitz, "Indeterminate Confinement: Letting the Therapy Fit the Harm," 123 *U. Pa. L. Rev.* 297 (1974).

confining the false positives is dubious justice. Ostensibly, those spotted as potential recidivists are being deprived of their liberty to prevent them from infringing on the rights of others. But, to the extent the prediction is wrong, that infringement would not have occurred. Granted, we are speaking of persons who have already been convicted of an offense. But the objection persists where a convicted individual is, on the basis of a mistaken prediction, being held *longer* than he otherwise would have been, had the prediction not influenced his sentence.

A forecast, while overpredicting, will also spot some persons who actually are dangerous (so-called true positives). Unless these are confined, innocent people will be hurt. But many more false positives may be confined than victims spared—for, as we just noted, the false positives are apt to outnumber the true by a substantial margin. And mistaken intervention may be especially objectionable, because the individual who is the false positive is being injured by the state under claim of right. No recognition can be accorded him for the wrong he suffers—as his confinement necessarily prevents him from demonstrating that he would have done no harm had he remained at large. The true positive's victim is likewise injured—but at least the injury is not treated by society as *rightfully* inflicted.* [15]

---

* The standard of proof in criminal trials is a somewhat parallel case in which more concern has traditionally been shown about the risks of erroneous intervention than about the risks of inaction. The common-law rule has been that guilt must be established beyond reasonable doubt. The Supreme Court in the 1970 Winship decision declared this standard was constitutionally mandated, describing it to be a fundamental requirement of fairness. The standard of proof in criminal trials—by affecting the chances of guilty (and possibly dangerous) persons to escape conviction—may influence the likelihood of future criminal victimization. But proof of guilt beyond reasonable doubt is a conception of fairness—not a rule of minimizing aggregate injury, derived through a one-to-one comparison of

Admittedly, there are other contexts where one's willingness to take risks diminishes as the gravity of the risk increases, irrespective of the number of false positives. One would withdraw the license of an airplane pilot who became ill if there was even a slight chance that his health could affect the safety of his passengers. But predictive restraint poses special ethical problems. The fact that the person's liberty is at stake reduces the moral acceptability of mistakes of overprediction. Moreover, one may question whether it is ever just to *punish* someone more severely for what he is expected to do, even if the prediction was accurate. The conventional notion of predictive restraint, preoccupied as it is with crime prevention, simply does not deal with such moral issues.

-----

harms to innocent accuseds with harms to prospective victims. Of course, even a "beyond reasonable doubt" standard permits conviction of some innocent persons. (And as recent Supreme Court rulings regarding jury unanimity indicate, how much certainty is actually required by the standard may be open to dispute.) But the Winship standard nevertheless suggests that when one must choose between mistaken intervention and mistaken non-intervention, the preference should ordinarily be for the latter when a person's liberty is at stake.

4

"Individualization"

"INDIVIDUALIZATION," the third major tenet, assumes that the disposition of the offender should be tailored to his particular case. To achieve individualization, sentencing judges and parole boards are supposed to have the widest discretion and their "expert" correctional judgments hampered by as few legal constraints as possible. The idea came into its own in the 1870s, when reformers argued against fixed penalties and in favor of indeterminate sentences.[1] It persists today—only now, the avowed aim is to afford flexibility for placing offenders into community treatment.[2]

The idea of individualization draws support from the two assumptions just discussed. If the purpose of the disposition is to treat, it follows that those skilled in rehabilitation should have flexibility to suit the treatment to the offender's need. And if the potential recidivist is to be restrained, the extent and duration of his restraint should be suited to the risk he poses to the public.

In the name of "individualization," sentencing judges in most jurisdictions have been given the widest leeway. When a convicted offender comes before a judge, the latter ordinarily has discretion either to release him outright on a suspended sentence, or place him on probation, or send him to prison, perhaps for years. (In Connecticut, for example, the judge's sentencing options for the offense of armed robbery range from unsupervised release to as many as twenty years' imprisonment.)[3] The judge's sentencing decision is not bound by any of the constraints which ordinarily govern his judicial work. He need not state his reasons for imposing a particular sentence, and usually no reasons are given. He is not required to follow any precedents; and his sentence is, generally, not reviewable by an appellate court.[4] While the sentence he imposes must not exceed the statutory maximum, the legislative maxima are customarily set so high as to be controlling in few but the most aggravated cases. Parole boards have similar sweeping powers. When a prisoner becomes eligible for parole (usually after about one third of his sentence has expired), the parole board has discretion to order his release or continue to hold him until expiration of sentence. Frequently, a parole board does not state any reasons for its decisions; no precedents are set; and no standards for release or continued incarceration are formulated.° [5] Moreover, the parole system makes the sentence indeterminate:

° The United States Parole Board, dealing with prisoners convicted of federal crimes, has announced a set of guidelines governing its release decisions; and, quite recently, California's parole board has done likewise. Most American jurisdictions, however, have yet to emulate these steps.

the imprisoned offender will not know what portion of his sentence he will actually serve in prison until the parole board finally makes its decision about release.

The most obvious drawback of allowing wide-open discretion in the name of "individualization" is the disparity it permits.[6] Judges whose sentencing decisions are unchecked by general standards are free to decide similar cases differently. A striking illustration emerged in a recent conference of federal trial judges of the Second Circuit, comprising New York, Connecticut, and Vermont.[7] The facts of numerous cases were selected from the files, and each of the fifty judges present was asked to state what sentences he would have imposed. The results, in some instances, were striking discrepancies. In one case, a crime that drew a three-year sentence from one judge drew a twenty-year term and a $65,000 fine from another. These disparities could not be attributed to differences in the cases being decided, since each judge was deciding on the identical set of assumed facts.

Such disparities cannot be attributed to judicial incompetence or bad faith. Judges who conscientiously strive for consistency in their own sentences may still differ in their respective sentencing philosophies, and those differences can lead to gross discrepancies of outcome, as Willard Gaylin has pointed out in his book *Partial Justice*. After interviewing numerous judges about their approaches to sentencing, and presenting four judges' views in detail, Gaylin concludes:

> each [judge] has a point of view, a set of standards and values, a bias, if you will, which will color, influence and direct the nature of his verdicts independently of the specific condition of the criminal being charged. . . . Five years is a maximum for

Judge Garfield; it is seen as a minimum for Judge Stone. Crimes against property are a rectification of the order of things, political actions, to Judge Ravitz; they are profound threats to the fabric of civilization to Judge Stone, and will be dealt with accordingly. These sets of values constitute bias in the non-pejorative sense—but bias nonetheless, and a bias that will influence equity and fairness in exactly the same way as naked bigotry does.[8]

It should also be borne in mind that courts, parole boards, and correctional agencies are bureaucracies: when these organizations are given such broad discretion, they tend to use it to deal with their management problems, irrespective of the purported aims of punishment. Courts will use their discretionary powers to control their caseloads; parole boards, to match the prison population to institutional bedspace. As Caleb Foote has noted in his study of parole in California:

> In the absence of normative standards . . . to reach a viable compromise of conflicting interests becomes the chief function of sentence-fixing. For the sentence-fixer, the characteristics of the criminal must compete with the necessities of placating . . . political pressure, displaying the necessary level of cooperation with law enforcement and prosecution, heeding the management interests of correctional bureaucracy, keeping a finger on the pulse of seething unrest in inmate populations, trying to maintain some degree of consistency with colleagues of widely divergent views, parrying the moves of those who would usurp his jurisdiction or manipulate him for their own ends, or compromising what he thinks are right solutions because of the constraints dictated by budget priorities or administrative policies over which he has no control.[9]

Amid this welter of pressing management concerns, reaching a disposition "suited" to the individual offender—the supposed aim of the discretion—is relegated to low priority. In Foote's words,

> Along this route the normal defendant-inmate—that unexceptional figure who represents 80 to 90 percent of the caseload— is a lonely and almost forgotten actor. Possessing neither substantive legal rights nor political muscle, he is the pawn in an interest conflict that he can influence only by chance and which he seldom understands.[10]

Where sentencing is indeterminate, these evils are compounded by the agonies of uncertainty. Inmates are kept for years in unbearable suspense about the most important matter in their lives—the time of their release. Not surprisingly, many prisoners regard the indeterminate sentence as perhaps the worst feature of prison existence.[11]

To cope with disparity, the remedy most frequently recommended is some form of review of individual judges' dispositions: appellate review of sentences, or else sentencing councils (where the trial judge, before imposing sentence, must submit the proposed disposition to two of his colleagues and obtain their views).[12] While they have been tried in some jurisdictions,[13] these procedures seldom have been accompanied by explicit substantive norms for sentencing.[14] No doubt, requiring the individual judge to obtain another judge's concurrence for his decision may be some check. (As Marvin Frankel notes of sentencing councils, "The individual extremes of sentencing inclination, both harsh and lenient, tend to be tempered.")[15] But unless the reviewing agency is prepared to state what norms should govern, sentencing review may be little more than the substitution of another official's unstructured discretion for that of the original judge.° [16]

° This was noted a number of years ago by the editors of the *Yale Law Journal* in a study of sentencing review in Connecticut. That state had instituted a system

Creating sentencing standards requires, first, a coherent conception of purposes.° If there are to be multiple aims in sentencing, priorities will have to be set: otherwise, it will be difficult to resist the temptation of leaving the reconciliation of competing purposes to the discretion of the judge or parole official in the individual case.† [17]

---

of appellate review of sentences, but failed to develop an intelligible body of precedents in its review decisions. The Yale study observed:

> To date, the most serious drawback to the [Connecticut Sentence Review] Division's effectiveness has been the idea that its primary function is to prevent "horrible sentencing examples." By seldom attempting to supply generally applicable sentencing criteria, the Division has overlooked its most significant potentialities and has lost the interest of other participants and decision-makers of the criminal process. Unless it assumes the role of an affirmative policy maker, *ad hoc*, instinctive decisions will continue to impede development in the field of sentencing.

° Without knowing what the aims are, it becomes difficult even to define precisely what disparity is. If two offenders convicted of the same offense receive different sentences, is that disparity? That depends on what other similarities and differences there are between the offenders and how these relate to the aims of punishment.

† This danger is illustrated in the Model Penal Code. The Code's statement of purposes lists several aims, but the drafters were not prepared to set priorities among them. The commentary states: "[The Code] does not undertake, however, to state a fixed priority among . . . the deterrence of potential criminals and the incapacitation and correction of the individual offender. These are all proper goals to be pursued in social action with respect to the offender, *one or another of which may call for the larger emphasis in a particular context or situation*" [emphasis added]. Once this critical question of priorities is left to be decided in the "particular context or situation," wide sentencing discretion follows almost inexorably—and that is manifest in the provisions of the Code.

II

Why Punish at All?
—The General
Justification
of Punishment

DECISIONS ABOUT the disposition of offenders after conviction are decisions about *punishing*—so our inquiry must be into the rationale of punishment.

We need, first, a simple working definition of punishment. *Punishment (for our purposes) means the infliction by the state of consequences normally considered unpleasant, on a person in response to his having been convicted of a crime.*° ¹ The definition of punishment ought not to be

---

° Dispositions in lieu of punishment fall slightly outside this definition but should nevertheless be considered a form of punishment. We are referring here to cases where there has been no formal finding of guilt but a *de facto* determination has been made that the person has, in fact, committed the offense; and his liberty is to be restricted as a consequence. An example is pretrial diversion, where charges are dropped against an accused defendant on condition that he limit his movements and/or participate in a treatment program.

We wish to stress that this working definition merely describes the use of the word "punishment" that is relevant to our analysis. (Our definition does not, for example, cover punishments for breaches of non-legal rules by parents or school authorities, although that is well within the normal use of the word.)

confused with its purposes. Is the measure unpleasant, and is it inflicted because of conviction for crime? If so, it qualifies as punishment regardless whether the purpose is to visit the offender with his deserts, deter him or others, incapacitate him from doing further harm, or provide him with treatment. The use of the old-fashioned word "punishment" should be a reminder of the painful nature of criminal sanctions, whatever their claimed objectives are.

In speaking of the rationale for punishment, we shall make use of a distinction derived from H. L. A. Hart's "Prolegomenon to the Principles of Punishment." [2] It is the distinction between (1) the *general justification*—that is, the reason or reasons why punishment should exist at all;° and (2) the rationale for *allocation*—that is, for distributing penalties of different severities among convicted offenders.† Our main concern is with allocation: whether (and why) one offender should be punished more or less severely than another. To develop an allocation theory, however, we must first examine the general justification, for it is the logically prior question: we need some idea of what the criminal sanction is supposed to accomplish before we can decide how much punishment different offenders should receive.

The terms "penalty" and "criminal sanction" will be used as synonymous with punishment, as defined here.

° The general justification should not only identify the aims of the institution of punishment but explain why the pursuit of those aims through punishment is *morally* justified. See K. G. Armstrong, "The Retributivist Hits Back," 70 *Mind* 471 (1961).

† Hart contrasts the general justification (Why should punishment exist?) with the *distribution* (Who may be punished and how much?). Distribution, in turn, he breaks down into *liability* (Under what circumstances may someone be punished?) and *amount* (How severely?). What we call "allocation" refers to the latter: the amount of punishment that may be inflicted on a convicted offender. As we are dealing with the post-conviction phase of the criminal justice system, questions of liability do not concern us directly.

5

General Deterrence

IT SEEMS almost a truism that criminals should be punished so there will be less crime. Why penalize murderers, speeders, and tax evaders, if not to deter killing, reckless driving, and tax fraud? This idea of general deterrence had prominence in the criminological literature of a century and a half ago: notably, in the writings of Jeremy Bentham.[1] By the end of the nineteenth century, however, the idea had come into disfavor: as criminologists began attributing crime to offenders' background or biological makeup, they became convinced that criminal behavior could not be influenced by the threat of penalties.[2] Yet, in recent years, largely under the influence of the Norwegian criminologist Johannes Andenaes,[3] the question has been reopened: general deterrence, never forsaken by law-enforcement officials, is again a topic of interest to scholars.

By "general deterrence," we mean the effect that a threat to punish has, in inducing people to refrain from prohibited conduct.° The warning that "speeders lose their licenses" is a deterrent if it causes some persons to obey the speed limits who otherwise might not have done so. The actual imposition of the punishment is a deterrent insofar as it makes the threat credible; in Oliver Wendell Holmes's words: "The law threatens certain pains if you do certain things. . . . If you persist in doing them, it has to inflict the pains in order that its threats may continue to be believed." [4] Essential to an understanding of the concept are these features:

• Even though a punishment does not alter the behavior of the particular individual who is penalized,† [5] it still is a general deterrent if the example of his punishment induces *other* persons to comply. This has been overlooked by some critics, who point to high recidivism rates among convicted offenders and assert that, since such persons have not been deterred, punishment has no general deterrent effect. But recidivism among convicted offenders shows only that they

° As the threat to punish may also provoke some persons to disobey, the threat is a deterrent, more precisely, if it induces more persons to obey than it provokes into disobeying. See Joseph Goldstein, "Psychoanalysis and Jurisprudence," 77 *Yale L. J.* 1053, 1071–2 (1968).

† General deterrence is sometimes contrasted with *individual* or *special* deterrence. The latter term is used to refer to the effect of punishment in inducing the individual who is penalized to refrain from further unlawful conduct. It rests on the hope that if sufficient unpleasantness is visited on the criminal, he will desist from crime in the future to avoid further pains. But, for our purposes, it is not a particularly useful concept. Insofar as special deterrence refers to trying to deter recidivism by penalizing second offenders more severely than first, it is—as Zimring and Hawkins point out in their book *Deterrence*—merely "a more rigorous application, to a particular group, of the principle of general deterrence." Insofar as it refers to some judges' practice of trying to tailor a penalty to intimidate a particular offender (e.g., giving a young offender on his first offense a "taste of jail"), it is not dissimilar to rehabilitation. That is, the offender is being subjected to a special regimen designed to alter his propensities to further criminal conduct.

have not been deterred, and indicates nothing about the effect of their punishment on the rest of the population. In the absence of any punishment, a much larger number of persons—who now refrain—might have committed crimes.* [6] General deterrence, it should be emphasized, is measured not just by the recidivism rate but by the *overall* offense rate (including first offenses).

• When it is asserted that a penalty is or is not a deterrent, one must ask: *Compared to what?* Consider the much debated question whether the death penalty "deters" murder. That question makes no sense unless one asks what the death penalty is being compared to. A number of studies have found that the death penalty yields no measurable reduction in homicide rates, when compared to sentences of prolonged imprisonment.[7] These studies, if correct, support the conclusion that the death penalty is no *greater* deterrent than long-term confinement. But were penalties reduced drastically or eliminated altogether, an increase in the rate of homicide might well result. To that extent, penalizing murder has some deterrent effect.

• The crime rate is affected not only by the threat of punishment but by numerous other social and economic factors as well. Thus, even if a change in crime rates is found to be associated with change in penalties, that does

---

* Another version of the same fallacy is the claim that general deterrence is a myth because offenders act impulsively and do not calculate the risks of punishment before breaking the law. Even if all actual offenders were to act impulsively, some more cautious individuals may have decided not to offend because of risk of being penalized. (And, as Andenaes points out, deterrence does not necessarily require conscious calculation. A person may refrain from tax cheating because he feels it wrong or because that is "not done" in his social group, but his or his group's attitudes may have been influenced indirectly by the fact that the conduct was punishable.)

not establish that the penalty change has had a deterrent effect unless one has controlled for such other possible influences on the crime rate. A number of statistical techniques exist for controlling for such other variables, but this has proven to be a troublesome issue.* [8]

WE ARE CONSIDERING HERE whether deterrence is reason for having *any* system of criminal sanctions at all. For that purpose, our evidentiary requirements are modest: only that (for some offenses, at least) the threat and imposition of punishment induces more compliance than if there were no punishment. We are persuaded that punishment does deter, at least in this minimal sense.

Most empirical studies of deterrence concern the effect on crime rates of varying the severity of penalties. The results have been mixed (as we will see later), with some

---

* The economist Gordon Tullock notes: "Statistically testing deterrence is not easy because the prospect of punishment obviously is not the *only* thing that affects the frequency with which crimes are committed. The crime rate varies with the degree of urbanization, the demographic composition of the population, the distribution of wealth, and many other circumstances. Some statistical technique is necessary to take care of these factors—and such techniques are now available. Using multiple regression (or, in a few cases, a complicated variant on the Chi-Square test), it is possible to put figures on each of these variables into the same equation and to see how much they influence the dependent variable which, in this case, is the rate of a specific crime. Although there are difficulties, this procedure will give a set of numbers called coefficients that are measures of the effect of *each* of the purported causative factors on the rate of commission of the given crime. If punishment deters crime, it will show up in these figures as a coefficient that is both significant and negative." However, not all statisticians share his optimism about the effectiveness of these techniques.

Time lag presents an additional problem. When a change in penalty shows no immediate impact on crime rates, it might still gradually alter people's perceptions of the wrongfulness of the behavior and thus have some effect on the rates over the long term. Yet the wider the time interval being considered, the harder it becomes to control for other variables that might influence the crime rates.

studies showing that increases in severity have a modest effect, and others showing no effect at all. But even if the crime rate is not particularly sensitive to variations in severity of the penalty, *a* penalty still may deter better than none. What is needed, then, is data comparing situations where conduct is penalized to situations where it is not. That kind of evidence is scarce (in part, because authorities have been loath to experiment with abolition of penalties). But some supporting data exist.

Some of the evidence is derived from instances where a penalty has been imposed and enforced for what previously were (in practice, at least) sanction-free acts. Britain's Road Safety Act of 1967 is an example. The Act created a new offense—driving with more than a stated amount of alcohol in the blood—and equipped police with portable breath-test kits to screen drivers suspected of intoxication. Conviction meant the revocation of license and a stiff fine, and the new law was widely publicized. Immediately after the legislation was enacted, the rate of nighttime traffic fatalities dropped sharply, suggesting a substantial decrease in drunken driving.[9] (Later the rate of fatalities increased somewhat from the low levels reached right after enactment—but did not return to the preenactment levels.) This evidence suggests that the imposition and enforcement of the penalty had some deterrent effect; as H. Laurence Ross points out:

> A possibility for obtaining such evidence [of deterrence exists] through the use of the quasi-experimental technique known as interrupted time-series analysis. This technique has been used successfully to demonstrate the validity of the belief that the British Road Safety Act of 1967 initially did produce deterrence of drinking and driving. The technique is based on the

expectation that if a cause-and-effect relationship exists between two variables, such as law and crashes, a change in the
causal variable will be associated with a simultaneous change in
the effect variable. In Britain it was shown that a significant
drop in motor-vehicle casualties occurred precisely at the time
of introduction of the new legislation. Furthermore, the drop in
casualties was greatest on weekend nights, when alcohol is
usually heavily involved in serious crashes, and not present
during weekday commuting hours, when alcohol is less often a
cause of such crashes.* [10]

(Other crimes, of course, may not be so responsive to the
threat of penalties. The deterrability of different criminal
behaviors varies with the kinds of people typically involved;
the strengths of their motives for crime; and the attractive-
ness of the available non-criminal alternatives. But for the
purposes of the present argument, it suffices if *some* kinds of
criminal conduct are deterrable.)

Another kind of evidence, although its probative value is
more problematical, is that obtained from "natural experi-
ments" such as police strikes, in which punishment for
certain crimes was effectively suspended for a period of
time. Perhaps the most famous such "natural experiment"
occurred in Copenhagen during the Second World War
when the entire municipal police force was arrested by the

---

* A study Ross subsequently conducted of similar legislation in Norway and
Sweden yielded negative results. Those, however, may have been attributable to
insufficiency of the data. As Ross notes:

The use of interrupted time-series analysis presupposes, among other things, the
existence of a valid measure of the effect variable for an extended period
preceding and following the change in the causal variable. Because the
Scandinavian *per se* laws were initiated relatively early in the history of the
automobile age and hence of motor-vehicle statistics it is not as easy to apply
this analysis to Sweden and Norway as to Britain, where the *per se* law had its
inception in 1967.

Nazis. Crime rates rose immediately: the rate of robberies, burglaries, and larcenies increased about tenfold, for without police, such offenses effectively became sanction-free.° [11] If such examples of non-enforcement can have these results, we might expect *a fortiori* that having no penalty at all could do the same.†

Such evidence is admittedly inconclusive. (It must be remembered that this question—whether some punishment deters more than none at all—has seldom been tested. This is in marked contrast to the state of evidence regarding the effectiveness of rehabilitative programs, where, as we have seen, there has been a great deal of experimentation with predominantly negative results.) But such evidence as exists for deterrence is supported by common experience. As Andenaes states, "It seems reasonably safe to evaluate the [deterrent] effects of punishment on a common sense basis. . . . it is still a fundamental fact of social life that the risk of unpleasant consequences is a very strong motivational factor for most people in most situations." [12] That the threat of penalties has some deterrent effect is something people experience in their everyday lives, whether it be when they

° The citizens of Copenhagen organized vigilante groups during that period. The vigilante groups were able to deal with crimes in which the offender could easily be identified by the victim, and rates for those crimes did not show any spectacular increase. But the vigilantes were not equipped to deal with offenses such as robbery, burglary, and larceny, where the offender was harder to trace and where specialized police work was called for. It was these crimes, which effectively became sanction-free in the absence of the police, that increased dramatically.

† In making inferences from the Copenhagen case, however, it should be noted that the presence of the police can have a deterrent effect independent of the threatened criminal sanctions. To the extent prospective offenders feel it inconvenient, unpleasant, or dangerous to be chased and apprehended by the police, that itself is a deterrent aside from the pains of the formal punishment that may follow being caught.

refrain from parking in a tow-away zone, avoid speeding on a patrolled highway, or comply with the directions of a police officer when they dislike doing so.

Assuming that punishment has some deterrent effect, it should be apparent why deterrence helps justify the existence of the criminal sanction. By means of the criminal law, the state proscribes various kinds of injurious conduct. The conduct is prohibited so that people will refrain from it. But were the prohibition not backed by sanctions, violations might become commonplace. The threat and imposition of punishment is called for in order to secure compliance—not full compliance, but more compliance than there might be were there no legal penalties at all.

Does that mean that deterrence is a *sufficient* justification for the existence of punishment? We think not, for reasons we shall explore next.

Desert

IN EVERYDAY thinking about punishment, the idea of desert figures prominently. Ask the person on the street why a wrongdoer should be punished, and he is likely to say that he "deserves" it. Yet the literature of penology seldom mentions the word. Instead, there is usually listed—along with the three traditional utilitarian aims of deterrence, incapacitation, and rehabilitation—a fourth aim of "retribution." We do not find "retribution" a helpful term. It has no regular use except in relation to punishment, so that one is precluded from learning about the concept from the word's use in other contexts. It also seems somewhat narrow. The Oxford English Dictionary, for example, defines retribution as "recompense for, or requital of evil done; return of evil";[1] this suggests a particular view of why punishment is deserved, namely that the offender should somehow be "paid back" for his wrong. Yet, as we will see presently, there are other explanations of deserved punishment which do not rely on this notion of requital-of-evil. Finally, the word is, perhaps through historical accident, burdened with pejorative associations.* [2]

We prefer the term "desert." Its cognate, "to deserve," is widely used: rewards, prizes, and grades, as well as punishments, are said to be deserved or undeserved. And the word "desert" is somewhat less emotionally loaded.

To say someone "deserves" to be rewarded or punished is to refer to his *past* conduct, and assert that its merit or demerit is reason for according him pleasant or unpleasant treatment.[3] The focus on the past is critical. That a student has written an outstanding paper is grounds for asserting that he deserves an award; but that the award will yield him or others future benefits (however desirable those might be) cannot be grounds for claiming he deserves it. The same holds for punishment: to assert that someone deserves to be punished is to look to his past wrongdoing as reason for having him penalized. This orientation to the past distinguishes desert from the other purported aims of punishment—deterrence, incapacitation, rehabilitation—which seek to justify the criminal sanction by its prospective usefulness in preventing crime.

It is important here to distinguish between the rationale

---

* Thus, the 1972 edition of the Model Sentencing Act states: "Sentences should not be based upon revenge and retribution." No explanation is supplied of why the idea of retribution should thus be summarily dismissed, or why it should be lumped together with revenge. The drafters of the Act assumed, apparently, that retribution is tantamount to vindictiveness toward offenders.

for punishing and the rationale for the underlying legal prohibitions. Concededly, the latter—the criminal law's substantive prohibitions—are forward-looking in their aim: murder is prohibited so that citizens will not kill one another. But the question is whether, once a violation has occurred, the basis for punishing the violator is still forward-looking, or is retrospective. Once a murder has taken place, is the only reason for penalizing the murderer to prevent subsequent violations by him or others? Or is there, at that point, a retrospective reason for punishing— that the murderer deserves to be punished? And if so, how is the notion of deserved punishment to be explained?

A useful place to begin is with Kant's explanation of deserved punishment, which he based on the idea of fair dealing among free individuals. To realize their own freedom, he contended, members of society have the reciprocal obligation to limit their behavior so as not to interfere with the freedom of others. When someone infringes another's rights, he gains an unfair advantage over all others in the society—since he has failed to constrain his own behavior while benefiting from other persons' forbearance from interfering with his rights. The punishment—by imposing a counterbalancing disadvantage on the violator— restores the equilibrium: after having undergone the punishment, the violator ceases to be at advantage over his non-violating fellows.° [4] (This righting-of-the-balance is not

___

° The Kantian argument presupposes that what violators are being punished for is the infringement of rules that safeguard the rights of *all* members of society including the violator's own rights. This raises a question that we shall explore further in Chapter 17—whether a desert-based justification for punishment, such as Kant's, can hold in a society whose penal system helps maintain a less-than-just social system.

a matter of preventing future crimes. Aside from any concern with prospective criminality, it is the violator's *past* crime that placed him in a position of advantage over others, and it is that advantage which the punishment would eliminate.) As Herbert Morris puts it in a recent restatement of the Kantian argument:

> A person who violates the rules has something others have—the benefits of the system [of mutual non-interference with others' rights]—but by renouncing what others have assumed, the burdens of self-restraint, he has acquired an unfair advantage. Matters are not even until this advantage is in some way erased. . . . Justice—that is punishing such individuals—restores the equilibrium of benefits and burdens. . . .[5]

Kant's theory, however, accounts only for the imposition of *some* kind of deprivation on the offender to offset the "advantage" he obtained in violating others' rights. It does not explain why that deprivation should take the peculiar form of punishment. Punishment differs from other purposefully inflicted deprivations in the moral disapproval it expresses: punishing someone conveys in dramatic fashion that his conduct was wrong and that he is blameworthy for having committed it.[*][6] Why, then, does the violator deserve to be *punished*, instead of being made to suffer another kind of deprivation that connotes no special moral stigma?

To answer this question it becomes necessary, we think, to focus specifically on the reprobation implicit in punishment and argue that *it* is deserved. Someone who infringes

---

[*] For a fuller account of the reprobative element in punishment, we refer the reader to Joel Feinberg's essay, "The Expressive Function of Punishment," in his book *Doing and Deserving*—as well as Henry M. Hart's fine essay, "The Aims of the Criminal Law."

the rights of others, the argument runs, does wrong and deserves blame for his conduct. It is because he deserves blame that the sanctioning authority is entitled to choose a response that expresses moral disapproval: namely, punishment. In other words, the sanction ought not only to deprive the offender of the "advantage" obtained by his disregard of the rules (the Kantian explanation); but do so in a manner that ascribes blame (the reprobative explanation).° [7]

This raises the question of what purpose the reprobation itself serves. Blaming persons who commit wrongful acts is, arguably, a way of reaffirming the moral values that were infringed.[7a] But to speak of reaffirming such values prompts the further question: Why should the violator be singled out for blame to achieve that end? The answer must ultimately be that the censure is itself deserved: that someone who is responsible for wrongdoing is blame*worthy* and hence may justly be blamed.

With this much preliminary explanation of the idea of deserved punishment, we turn to the main question: whether desert is necessary to justify the criminal sanction.

From Deterrence to Desert. We have already suggested one reason for punishing: deterrence. The criminal sanction is

---

° Whether a reprobative theory could be the *only* explanation of deserved punishment is more problematical. Feinberg suggests that punishment has two analytically separable aspects: (1) infliction of pains, and (2) symbolic condemnation. A reprobative theory accounts for why the offender deserves to be condemned, but, Feinberg suggests, this condemnatory function could conceivably be achieved by a dramatic public ritual—and if so, the infliction of pains remains to be accounted for. It may be that *both* the Kantian and the reprobative explanation are required; the former to explain why the offender is deserving of some kind of deprivation, and the latter to explain why it should take the form of public reprobation that is characteristic of punishment.

called for to prevent certain kinds of injurious conduct. Why is it not sufficient to rely on that simple argument— and get on with deciding how punishment should rationally be allocated? Why bring in desert, with all its philosophical perplexities?

On utilitarian assumptions, deterrence would indeed suffice. The main utilitarian premise is (roughly) that a society is rightly ordered if its major institutions are arranged to achieve the maximum aggregate satisfaction and the minimum aggregate suffering.[8] On this premise, punishment would be justified if it deterred sufficiently— because, in sum, more suffering would be prevented through the resulting reduction in crime than is caused by making those punished suffer. Our difficulty is, however, that we doubt the utilitarian premise: that the suffering of a few persons is made good by the benefits accruing to the many. A free society, we believe, should recognize that an individual's rights—or at least his most important rights— are prima facie entitled to priority over collective interests.* [9] This idea has been best expressed, perhaps, by the philosopher John Rawls in the opening pages of his *Theory of Justice.* "Each person," he writes, "possesses an inviolabil-

---

* Which rights of the individual are of sufficient importance to be accorded this special priority can be a more difficult question. Is it all his rights, including, say, the right to hold and dispose of property? (The philosopher Robert Nozick has assumed so, and has constructed an argument for a minimal state on that basis.) Or should only certain "fundamental" rights be given this preferred status, leaving other individual interests, possibly including property, open to being distributed according to the utilitarian principle of the greatest good for the greatest number? (Peter Singer has made this suggestion, in a recent review of Nozick's book.)

But this problem of which rights are sufficiently important—perplexing as it may be when dealing with issues of economic justice—poses less difficulty for us. For the interests which punishment may intrude upon include the most important the individual can possibly have: his liberty. If *any* interests of the individual should be entitled to priority over collective interests, this surely should be among them.

ity founded on justice that even the welfare of society as a whole cannot override . . . justice denies that the loss of freedom for some is made right by a greater good shared by others. It does not allow that the sacrifices imposed on a few are outweighed by the larger sum of advantages enjoyed by many." [10]

Given this assumption of the primacy of the individual's fundamental rights, no utilitarian account of punishment, deterrence included, can stand alone. While deterrence explains why most people benefit from the existence of punishment, the benefit to the many is not by itself a just basis for depriving the offender of his liberty and reputation. Some other reason, then, is needed to explain the suffering inflicted on the offender: that reason is desert. The offender may justly be subjected to certain deprivations because he deserves it; and he deserves it because he has engaged in wrongful conduct—conduct that does or threatens injury and that is prohibited by law. The penalty is thus not just a means of crime prevention but a merited response to the actor's deed, "rectifying the balance" in the Kantian sense and expressing moral reprobation of the actor for the wrong. In other words: while deterrence accounts for why punishment is socially useful, desert is necessary to explain why that utility may justly be pursued at the offender's expense.° [11]

° The traditional objection to purely utilitarian theories of punishment has been that they justify too much: that if the prevention of crime is the sole aim, why not also punish the innocent if that will prevent crime more effectively? H. L. A. Hart has pointed out, however, that this objection can be met if one is careful to observe the distinction between the general justifying aim of punishment and the rules for its distribution. Even if a utilitarian view is espoused of why the criminal sanction should exist in the first place, Hart suggests, the rules for distributing punishments should still (in the interests of fairness) prohibit penalizing those who have

In speaking thus of desert as necessary to the justification of punishment, we are not referring to channeling theories such as Oliver Wendell Holmes's:[12] that ordinary citizens believe wrongdoers should suffer, and would resort to private vengeance were the law not to punish. Perhaps the restraint of vengeance is an important function of the criminal sanction, but this is another utilitarian claim: that there will be less social disruption if offenders are punished by the state rather than left to private retaliation.° What still must be explained is why, in thus benefiting society, it is just to deprive offenders of *their* rights by penalizing them. To answer that question, a moral claim must be made: not that the public thinks punishment is deserved and will do harm if its opinion is disregarded; but that punishment *is* deserved.

The Converse: From Desert to Deterrence. The route of argument just taken is the more familiar in current philosophical literature on punishment: begin with deterrence as a reason for punishing, then consider whether it must be supplemented by desert. However, the logic can be reversed: one can start by relying on the idea of desert. But again, the interdependence of the two concepts—desert and deterrence—will quickly become apparent.

Desert may be viewed as reason in itself for creating a

---

committed no unlawful act. Our criticism of utilitarianism is somewhat different: we are not speaking of who should be punished (distribution) but of why anyone ever should be punished (general justification). We are suggesting that, given our assumption about the primacy of individual rights, the benefits accruing to society simply do not justify depriving anyone (even violators) of their fundamental rights: that it is essential to the very existence of the criminal sanction that the violator deserves to be punished.

° Offenders would also suffer less, to the extent that the state's punishments are not so drastic as private vengeance would be. But the question at issue here is why offenders should be made to suffer *at all*.

social institution. This is evident in the case of rewards. Most societies, including our own, reward those who have done deeds of special merit. Rewards may serve utilitarian ends (e.g., as an incentive for desired conduct); but, even disregarding such utility, a case for rewarding merit can be made simply on the grounds that it is deserved. Good work and good acts ought to be acknowledged for their own sake, and rewards express that acknowledgment. A parallel argument might be made for punishment:° those who violate others' rights deserve to be punished, on the Kantian and reprobative grounds just discussed. A system of punishment is justified, the argument runs, simply because it is deserved.

However, there are countervailing moral considerations.† An important counterconsideration is the principle of not deliberately causing human suffering where it can possibly be avoided. With rewards, this principle does not stand in the way: for rewards per se do not inflict pain (other than the possible discomforts of envy). It is otherwise with punishment: while wrongdoers deserve punishment, it is necessarily painful. Arguably, the principle against inflicting suffering should, in the absence of other considerations, override the case for punishing based on wrongdoers' deserts.

It is at this point in the argument that the idea of

° We mention the parallel of rewards merely to illustrate the structure of the argument. Obviously, rewards differ from punishments in important respects (e.g., they are not visited compulsorily on the recipient), so that one might argue for a system of rewards on the basis of desert without being compelled to argue similarly for punishment.

† To say someone deserves to be treated in a certain manner is to claim *a* reason for so treating him—but still allows one to conclude that he should not be treated as he deserves if there are sufficient countervailing reasons.

deterrence becomes critical—for it can supply an answer to the countervailing concern about the infliction of suffering. When punishment's deterrent effect is taken into account, it may cause less misery than not punishing would. Moreover, not only might total misery be reduced, but its distribution would be more acceptable: fewer innocent persons will be victimized by crimes, while those less deserving—the victimizers—will be made to suffer instead. Deterrence thus tips the scales back in favor of the penal sanction. To state the argument schematically:

Step 1: Those who violate others' rights deserve punishment. That, of itself, constitutes a prima-facie justification for maintaining a system of criminal sanctions.

Step 2: There is, however, a countervailing moral obligation of not deliberately adding to the amount of human suffering. Punishment necessarily makes those punished suffer. In the absence of additional argument, that overrides the case for punishment in step 1.

Step 3: The notion of deterrence, at this point, suggests that punishment may prevent more misery than it inflicts—thus disposing of the countervailing argument in step 2. With it out of the way, the prima-facie case for punishment described in step 1—based on desert—stands again.

The case for punishing differs, then, from the case for rewards. With rewards, it is sufficient to argue that they are deserved: since rewards are not painful, there is no need to point to their collateral social usefulness to excuse the misery they cause. Punishments, likewise, are deserved; but, given the overriding concern with the infliction of pain, the notion of deterrence has to be relied upon as well.

THE FOREGOING shows the interdependence of the twin concepts of deterrence and desert. When one seeks to justify the criminal sanction by reference to its deterrent utility, desert is called for to explain why that utility may justly be pursued at offenders' expense. When one seeks to justify punishment as deserved, deterrence is needed to deal with the countervailing concern about the suffering inflicted. The interdependence of these two concepts suggests that the criminal sanction rests, ultimately, on *both*.

III

How Severely to Punish?—The Allocation of Penalties

HAVING DISCUSSED the general justification of punishment, we turn to our central concern: the allocation of penalties among convicted offenders.

Deciding how much to punish is an agonizing process in which conflicting aspirations compete. The best one can do is decide which aspirations, on balance, appear to be most important—and build one's theory on them. Any such theory will necessarily oversimplify the moral dilemmas the decision-maker faces. Yet a rationale for allocation can bring a sense of priorities into practical decisions about punishment, difficult as these always will be.

In our discussion of the general justification in the preceding section, we relied on two conceptions—deterrence and desert. In the allocation of penalties, desert becomes preeminent. We will argue that the distribution of penalties among convicted offenders should be decided chiefly by reference to the seriousness of the offense of which the offender has been convicted and the number and seriousness of his prior convictions.

7

Deterrence and Allocation

DETERRENCE, we contend, has a less central role to play in allocating penalties than in justifying the existence of the criminal sanction.

In arguing that deterrence is a reason for punishment's existence, we had modest requirements for evidence: it sufficed if, for certain offenses at least, some penalty deterred better than none. But if deterrence is to be the basis for allocating penalties, the requirements for evidence become more exacting: it becomes necessary to know, for different categories of offenses, by how much the crime rate is affected as the penalty varies.

Two hundred years ago, Cesare Beccaria suggested that increasing the *certainty* of punishment yields higher deterrent returns than increasing its *severity*.[1] Recent empirical studies have suggested that, for some categories of crime, the rate of infractions does, indeed, vary with the likelihood of the offender's being apprehended and punished.[2] Less is known, however, about the influence of severity on the rate of crime.

Most earlier studies showed little or no discernible deterrent effect from varying the severity. The best known of these is the research on the death penalty conducted some years ago by the sociologist Thorsten Sellin. Sellin's investigations showed no appreciable difference in homicide rates between states that had the death penalty and adjacent states that had abolished it. Similarly, no change was found in homicide rates within a single jurisdiction before and after that sanction had been abolished (or restored).[3] Negative results were also reported in an elaborate investigation of bad check laws in Nebraska conducted by F. K. Beutel.[4]

Recently, economists have tried to measure the deterrent effects of severity by applying classical economic theory and econometric formulas to crime data, and some positive results have been reported.[5] For example, Isaac Ehrlich, a University of Chicago economist, applied an econometric model to multi-state data for the seven F.B.I. index crimes and found that the severity of penalties had some influence on crime rates.[6] Even these econometric studies generally substantiate Beccaria's thesis, however: when severity was found to affect crime rates, the effect was considerably weaker than that of the likelihood of being punished.[7] And these studies generally suffer from the defect that the data base used—official crime statistics—is far from reliable.[*]

---

[*] The distortions that may result from using official crime statistics have been described by David Greenberg, formerly of our Committee's staff:

The . . . reliance on official sources for crime statistics is another possible source

It is possible—as several researchers have suggested—that when severity increases, its deterrent returns tend to diminish:° [8] whereas some deterrence will be achieved when formerly unpunished conduct is subjected to a modest penalty, a severe penalty is apt to show little more effect than a modest one. (Once the penalty progresses beyond moderate severity, potential offenders may be insensitive to further increases because they are gambling on not getting caught.)† [9] But that hypothesis, even if true, does not supply

---

of error. . . . While under-reporting in itself would not distort the correlation coefficients obtained from official data, systematic variations might. [For example,] if penalties are widely regarded as excessive, or if arrests and convictions are obtained through law enforcement procedures that evoke resentment and hostility, victims might be less willing to report crimes. Where this is so, deterrent effects would be overstated.

David F. Greenberg: "Theft, Rationality and Deterrence Research," Department of Sociology, New York University, July 1975 (unpublished). The Greenberg paper also contains other criticisms of current deterrence studies' methodology.

° Such a hypothesis of diminishing returns would help reconcile some of the evidence we touched upon. Where the conduct was not penalized at all, imposing a penalty was found to have some deterrent effect, as was true of the British Road Safety Act mentioned in Chapter 5. But where, as in many of the studies mentioned in the present chapter, the conduct was substantially punishable already, additional severity had a less clear-cut effect.

The hypothesis of diminishing returns of severity is also suggested by economists' notion of discounting future costs. As Ehrlich states, "Since punishment always follows the commission of crime (and the criminal payoff collected thereupon), and is often extended over a long period of time (as in the case of imprisonment) following an offender's conviction, the *discounted* (present-equivalent) monetary value of the delayed costs of crime is necessarily lower than, and less than proportionally related to, their future value if the discount rate is positive." For this discounting principle to apply, however, the increment in severity must be deferred in time—as when the duration of imprisonment is increased.

† For this reason, perhaps, the effectiveness of increasing severity may depend on the probability of apprehension and punishment. Where—as in the real world—this probability is low, committing a crime may be an acceptable risk (at least for those not averse to risk), notwithstanding the great severity of the penalty in the unlikely event of being caught. Were enforcement much more efficient, the penalty level might begin to make more difference. As sociologist Charles Tittle

the specific answers needed—it does not tell one at what levels of severity, for different kinds of crimes, this phenomenon of diminishing returns sets in.

Were the data to become available, there remains the still more perplexing problem of how they should be applied in decisions to punish.

At best, empirical research can tell one how much the rate of an offense will be affected by changes in the severity of the penalty: increasing the penalty by so much will (or will not) produce such-and-such a reduction in the crime rate. But, knowing that, does one then opt for the lower or the higher penalty? That is not an empirical question but a value judgment—of how important it is to prevent the conduct, and at what cost in suffering to the individuals who are to be punished.

The traditional utilitarian approach to the question of how severely to punish is: weigh the "costs" of punishing against the deterrent returns of the penalty. (The idea was originally Bentham's, but it persists today—especially in economic models for calculating optimum penalties.)° [10] While punishment prevents harm by deterring crimes, it also creates harm by making punished offenders suffer—and their pains must also be taken into account. The optimum penalty, according to this theory, is that which maximizes the aggregate benefits (crimes prevented) while minimizing

---

states, "Severity of sanctions may come into play only after certain levels of certainty have been achieved." The truth of Tittle's conjecture remains unconfirmed, however; and its utility may be questionable—as severity may influence crime rates only at levels of enforcement efficiency well beyond what can practicably be expected in the foreseeable future.

° It is also suggested in the American Friends Service Committee's report, *Struggle for Justice*, and that is one of the few major points where we disagree with that thoughtful book.

the costs (including the pain inflicted on punished offenders).

Besides yielding some anomalous results,° this cost-benefit solution seems to us conceptually flawed. Punishment is not simply another "cost" to be inflicted upon some persons, justifiable insofar as it produces more total good than harm. When speaking earlier about why punishment should exist at all, we argued that its deterrent usefulness was not sufficient justification—that the *justice* of making punished individuals suffer must also be accounted for. The same is true for allocation: to the extent that the penalty is more severe than just, its aggregate social utility should not warrant the added intrusion. How, then, can one determine what amount of punishment is just for a given offense? That question has to be confronted explicitly. The weakness of cost-benefit reckonings is that they turn one's attention away from this moral issue, and toward the all-too-reassuring and familiar task of toting up costs and benefits.

To deal with such questions of justice, we shall leave deterrence for the moment and examine the role of desert in allocating penalties. We return to deterrence later, when we consider the overall dimensions of a penalty scale.

° On certain states of the evidence, this theory could justify severe penalties for seemingly minor crimes or vice versa.

Suppose the data showed that a certain type of petty larceny would sharply decline when a severe penalty was invoked against a very few offenders. Traditional utilitarian theory would support using the severe penalty, if the aggregate harm prevented (inconvenience to many individual victims) exceeded the aggregate pain inflicted (a severe sanction imposed only on a few offenders).

Conversely, suppose the data showed that some serious crimes (e.g., rape) showed little sensitivity to changes in the penalty, with a severe punishment deterring no more efficiently than a quite lenient one. Since no added benefit (lower crime rate) would then be obtained by the additional severity, the theory could require the imposition of the lenient penalty—even if that meant ranking the penalty below that for much less serious (but more deterrable) infractions.

8

The Principle of Commensurate Deserts

IF ONE ASKS how severely a wrongdoer deserves to be punished, a familiar principle comes to mind: *Severity of punishment should be commensurate with the seriousness of the wrong.* Only grave wrongs merit severe penalties; minor misdeeds deserve lenient punishments. Disproportionate penalties are undeserved—severe sanctions for minor wrongs or vice versa. This principle has variously been called a principle of "proportionality" or "just deserts"; we prefer to call it *commensurate deserts,* a phrase that better suggests the concepts involved. In the most obvious cases, the principle seems a truism (who would wish to imprison shoplifters for life, or let murderers off with small fines?). Yet, whether and how it should be applied in allocating punishments has been in dispute.

IN AN EARLIER ERA, the principle of commensurate deserts had a firmly established place in criminal jurisprudence. Cesare Beccaria's *Of Crimes and Punishments*, written in 1764, gives it much emphasis.[1] Punishments, he stated, should be carefully graded to correspond with the gravity of offenses. To Beccaria and his followers,[2] the principle was grounded on common-sense notions of fairness—and on utilitarian considerations as well: if penalties were not scaled commensurately with offenses, criminals, it was feared, would as soon commit grave crimes as minor ones. Criminal codes of the era—such as the French Code of 1791 [3] and the Bavarian Code of 1813 [4]—reflected this conception. The framers of the original New Hampshire Constitution considered the principle so central to a fair and workable system of criminal justice that they embodied it in the state's Bill of Rights.* [5]

Yet, with the rise of the rehabilitative ideology in the nineteenth century, the principle of commensurate deserts went into eclipse.[6]

One school of thought dismissed the principle entirely. Desert was seen as relevant only before conviction—when it was being decided whether the violator had acted with the requisite degree of culpability to be held criminally liable. After conviction, the seriousness of his offense was not to be considered at all; his punishment was instead to be determined by his need for treatment and his likelihood of

---

* The 1783 New Hampshire Constitution provides: "All penalties ought to be proportioned to the nature of the offense. No wise legislator will affix the same punishment to the crimes of theft, forgery, and the like, which they do to those of murder and treason. When the same undistinguishing severity is exerted against all offenses, the people are led to forget the real distinction in the crimes themselves, and to commit the most flagrant with as little compunction as they do those of the lightest dye." Several other states included similar provisions in their constitutions.

returning to crime. The Model Sentencing Act (in both its 1963 and its 1972 versions) takes this view.[7] The Act does not provide scaled maximum penalties for different categories of offenses. Instead, it gives the judge discretion to impose up to a five-year sentence on an offender convicted of any felony: within this limit, irrespective of the character of the offense, the judge is supposed to fix a sentence on the basis of the risk the offender poses to society.

Others have not been quite so uncompromising, conceding a residual significance to the seriousness of the offense. Most criminal codes provide maximum penalties for different offenses, ranked according to some approximate scale of gravity. But these legislative maxima are set so much higher than the sentences ordinarily expected that they have not much influence on actual dispositions.[*] [8] The American Law Institute's Model Penal Code recommends also that the judge should not set the sentence so low as to "depreciate the seriousness of the offense";[9] the Code fails, however, to clarify how much weight should be given this factor of "depreciating the seriousness" as contrasted with other possible goals of sentencing. Although H. L. A. Hart comments briefly in his "Prolegomenon" on how the principle serves as a constraint of fairness,[†] [10] his thoughts on this subject (unlike so much else in his influential essay) did not stimulate much further interest. The justification for the principle; the weight to be assigned it as contrasted with

---

[*] See Chapter 4. A few courts have invalidated penal statutes authorizing the imposition of extraordinarily harsh penalties for minor offenses; see, e.g., the California Supreme Court's 1972 decision in *In re Lynch*, invalidating as "cruel or unusual" punishment a penalty of up to life imprisonment for the crime of indecent exposure.

[†] See footnote on p. 70.

other possible aims of punishing; the meaning of "seriousness"; and the relevance of the principle to the knotty question of sentencing discretion—all these have remained largely unexplored until quite recently.[11]

THE PRINCIPLE looks retrospectively to the seriousness of the offender's past crime or crimes. "Seriousness" depends both on the harm done (or risked) by the act and on the degree of the actor's culpability. (When we speak of the seriousness of "the crime," we wish to stress that we are *not* looking exclusively to the act, but also to how much the actor can be held to blame for the act and its consequences.) If the offender had a prior criminal record at the time of conviction, the number and gravity of those prior crimes should be taken into account in assessing seriousness. (The meaning of "seriousness" and the significance of a prior criminal record will be explored more fully later.)

THE PRINCIPLE of commensurate deserts, in our opinion, is a requirement of justice;° [12] thus:

· The principle has its counterpart in common-sense notions of equity which people apply in their everyday lives. Sanctions disproportionate to the wrong are seen as manifestly unfair—whether it be an employee being fired for a minor rule infraction to make an example of him, or a school

---

° There also are utilitarian arguments for the principle (e.g., Bentham's argument that penalties should be proportioned so as "to induce a man to choose always the least mischievous of two offences"). But were utilitarian arguments the only basis for the principle, it could be disregarded in those classes of cases where there would be still greater social benefits in so doing. We want to argue that departures from the principle—even when they would serve utilitarian ends—inevitably sacrifice justice.

inflicting unequal punishments on two children for the same misdeed.

• The principle ensures, as no utilitarian criterion of allocation can, that the rights of the person punished not be unduly sacrificed for the good of others. When speaking earlier of the general justification of punishment, we argued that the social benefits of punishing do not alone justify depriving the convicted offender of his rights: it is also necessary that the deprivation be deserved. A similar argument holds for allocation. When the offender is punished commensurately with his offense, the state is entitled to sacrifice his rights to that degree because that is what he deserves. A utilitarian theory of allocation (one based on deterrence, for instance) could lead to punishing the offender more severely than he deserves if the net benefits of so doing were to outweigh the costs. The excess in severity may be useful for society, but that alone should not justify the added intrusion into the rights of the person punished.* [13]

---

* H. L. A. Hart has argued that even were one to take a wholly utilitarian view of the general justification of punishment (e.g., that punishment exists to deter), one *still* would be obliged as a matter of fairness to observe a proportion between the seriousness of the offense and the severity of the punishment. His words are worth quoting:

> The further principle that different kinds of offence of different gravity (however that is assessed) should not be punished with equal severity is one which like other principles of Distribution may qualify the pursuit of our General Aim and is not deducible from it. Long sentences of imprisonment might effectually stamp out car parking offences, yet we think it wrong to employ them; *not* because there is for each crime a penalty "naturally" fitted to its degree of iniquity (as some Retributionists in General Aim might think); not because we are convinced that the misery caused by such sentences (which might indeed be slight because they would rarely need to be applied) would be greater than that caused by the offences unchecked (as a Utilitarian might argue). The guiding principle is that of a proportion within a system of penalties between those imposed for different offences where these have a distinct place in a commonsense scale of gravity.

• The principle ensures that offenders are not treated as more (or less) blameworthy than is warranted by the character of the offense. Punishment, as we noted earlier, imparts blame. A criminal penalty is not merely unpleasant (so are taxes and conscription): it also connotes that the offender acted wrongfully and is reprehensible for having done so.° The offender, in other words, is being treated *as though he deserves* the unpleasantness that is being inflicted on him. That being the case, it should be inflicted only to the degree that it is deserved.

Where standards of criminal liability are concerned, this is a familiar point—for Henry M. Hart made it nearly two decades ago in his defense of the criminal law's *mens rea* requirements.[14] Since punishment characteristically ascribes blame, he contended, accidental violations should not be punished—because they are not blameworthy.

What is often overlooked, however, is that the same holds true after conviction. By then, it has been decided that the offender deserves punishment—but the question *how much* he deserves remains. The severity of the penalty carries implications of degree of reprobation. The sterner the

---

Our argument differs somewhat from Hart's because we suggest (in Chapter 6) that desert is also essential to the general justification. On our view, it follows *a fortiori* that desert should also govern the distribution of penalties.

° The unpleasantness of punishment and its reprobative connotations are inextricably mixed. Being severely punished—sent to prison, for example—signifies a high degree of blame; but being imprisoned is painful not only because one is being deprived of one's freedom of movement but because one is being so deprived as a symbol of obloquy.

The reprobative connotations of punishment stem, essentially, from the context in which it is imposed—from the fact that it is inflicted mainly on persons who have intentionally done forbidden acts (acts that in most instances also strongly offend the society's moral norms). As long as that is the occasion for punishment, reprobation would be present even if the authorities were to try to label the disposition "preventive" or "therapeutic."

punishment, the greater the implicit blame: sending someone away for several years connotes that he is more to be
condemned than does jailing him for a few months or
putting him on probation. In the allocation of penalties,
therefore, the crime should be sufficiently serious to merit
the implicit reprobation. The principle of commensurate
deserts ensures this. If the principle is not observed, the
degree of reprobation becomes inappropriate. Where an
offender convicted of a minor offense is punished severely,
the blame which so drastic a penalty ordinarily carries will
attach to him—and unjustly so, in view of the not-so-very
wrongful character of the offense. (This last argument, it
should be noted, does not presuppose the general justification of punishment which we urged earlier. Whatever the
ultimate aim of the criminal sanction—even if one were to
defend its existence on purely utilitarian grounds—punishment still *in fact* ascribes blame to the person. Hence the
severity of the penalty—connoting as it does the degree of
blame ascribed—ought to comport with the gravity of the
infraction.)° 15

Equity is sacrificed when the principle is disregarded,
even when done for the sake of crime prevention. Suppose
there are two kinds of offenses, *A* and *B*, that are of

° This argument would not apply, admittedly, to a ritual so different from
punishment that the reprobative overtones were largely absent. An example might
be a purely preventive system that isolated "dangerous" persons regardless of
whether any prohibited act was found to have been committed. But such a system
would be open to other kinds of objections. Many of those confined would be false
positives. Worse still, an individual would have no assurance that he can remain at
liberty as long as he takes care to comply with the rules; his continued freedom
"would depend not upon his voluntary acts, but upon his *propensities* for future
conduct as they are seen by the state . . . his liberty would depend upon
predictive determinations which he would have little ability to foretell, let alone
alter by his own choices" (Emphasis in original).

approximately equal seriousness; but that offense *B* can more effectively be deterred through the use of a severe penalty. Notwithstanding the deterrent utility of punishing offense *B* more severely, the objection remains that the perpetrators of that offense are being treated as though they are more blameworthy than the perpetrators of offense *A*—and that is not so if the crimes are of equivalent gravity.

It is sometimes suggested that the principle of commensurate deserts sets only an upper limit on severity—*no more* than so much punishment.[16] We disagree. Imposing only a slight penalty for a serious offense treats the offender as *less* blameworthy than he deserves. Understating the blame depreciates the values that are involved: disproportionately lenient punishment for murder implies that human life—the victim's life—is not worthy of much concern; excessively mild penalties for official corruption denigrate the importance of an equitable political process. The commensurateness principle, in our view, bars disproportionate leniency as well as disproportionate severity.° [17]

Norval Morris has recently suggested that the principle sets only broad upper and lower limits[18]—and that, within those limits, the sentence should be determined on utilitarian grounds (e.g., deterrence). Again, we do not agree. Concededly, it is easier to discern gross excess in lenience or severity than to decide on a specific proportion between a crime and its punishment. But, as we have seen, the

---

° If the concern is not to allow the punishment to become so lenient as to depreciate the blameworthiness of the conduct, the penalty scale could still be kept to modest dimensions. It would not be necessary, for example, to inflict as much suffering on the offender as he did on the victim ("an eye for an eye"), as the penalty would merely have to impart blame enough to express a sense of the gravity of the crime. Such issues—of how "commensurate" severity may be gauged—will be considered at greater length in Chapter 11.

principle is infringed when disparate penalties are imposed on equally deserving offenders. If *A* and *B* commit a burglary under circumstances suggesting similar culpability, they deserve similar punishments; imposing unequal sanctions on them for utilitarian ends—even within the outer bounds of proportionality Morris proposes—still unjustly treats one as though he were more to blame than the other. Our view of the principle as requiring equal treatment for the equally deserving has important implications for the structure of a penalty system, as we will see.

It has also been objected (by the drafters of the Model Sentencing Act, for instance)[19] that applying the principle in sentencing decisions would aggravate disparities, given judges' divergent views of the seriousness of offenses. But that holds true only if, as in current practice, the assessment of seriousness is left to the discretion of the individual judge. The principle has to be consistently applied; and consistent application requires (as we will elaborate later) the articulation of standards and the placing of limits on individual decision-makers' discretion.

THE commensurate-deserts principle may sometimes conflict with other objectives: for example, if an offense is not serious but can better be deterred by a severe penalty, commensurate deserts and deterrence may suggest divergent sentences. To deal with such conflicts, it becomes necessary to decide what priority should be given the principle.

We think that the commensurate-deserts principle should have priority over other objectives in decisions about how much to punish. The disposition of convicted offenders should be commensurate with the seriousness of their offenses, even if greater or less severity would promote other goals. For the principle, we have argued, is a requirement of justice, whereas deterrence, incapacitation, and rehabilitation are essentially strategies for controlling crime. The priority of the principle follows from the assumption we stated at the outset: the requirements of justice ought to constrain the pursuit of crime prevention.

In giving the principle this priority, we need not claim the priority to be absolute: perhaps (as we will discuss in Chapter 15) there are some unusual cases where it will be necessary to vary from the deserved sentence. But the principle derives its force from the fact that it applies *unless* special reasons for departing from it are shown: the burden rests on him who would deviate from the commensurate sentence.

Giving commensurate deserts this prominence will have practical usefulness in sorting out decisions about punishment. An often-repeated theme in the literature has been that the offender's disposition should be decided by "balancing" the different aims of punishment: the diverse considerations—rehabilitation, predictive restraint, deterrence, possibly desert as well—are to be weighed against each other, to yield an optimum penalty in the offender's particular case.[20] When the different objectives are in conflict, however, saying they should be "balanced" against each other does not offer a principled way of resolving the issue. One escapes this difficulty by giving the commensurate-deserts principle prima-facie controlling effect. No longer would it be necessary to weigh these conflicting objectives in each case. Rather, the disposition would be presumed to be—unless there are overriding grounds for deciding otherwise—the one which satisfies the principle of commensurate deserts. Instead of juggling competing rationales to reach a decision, one has a workable starting point.

9

Seriousness of Crimes

HAVING ARGUED that the severity of the penalty should depend on the seriousness of the offense, we face the question: How should "seriousness" be judged?

With the rise of the rehabilitative ideology in the last century, the concept of seriousness ceased to hold much interest—since the offender ostensibly was being treated, not punished as he deserved. Seriousness becomes a critical question, however, if the principle of commensurate deserts is given prominence.

Developing criteria for seriousness calls for a full study in itself. Here we shall only touch briefly upon some of the issues: our comments are meant to suggest that something *can* be said about seriousness—and that this inquiry is worth pursuing.

Legislatures have long been making judgments of seriousness in the maximum penalties they set. The prescribed maxima in criminal codes usually are scaled according to the legislature's sense of the gravity of the offenses involved, with murder and other heinous crimes carrying the greatest maximum penalties, and petty larcenies and other minor infractions the least. But these statutory limits are so seldom decisive in actual sentencing decisions* that drafters have had little need to consider questions of relative seriousness with much care.

Of greater interest are empirical studies that have been made of popular perceptions of the seriousness of offenses. The pioneering study was conducted in the 1960s by sociologists Thorsten Sellin and Marvin Wolfgang at the University of Pennsylvania.[1] They took a group of judges, college students, and policemen and asked them to rate the "seriousness" of various offenses on an eleven-point rating scale. The investigators found considerable agreement on the ranking of seriousness of crimes. The Sellin-Wolfgang findings were subsequently criticized on the grounds that their sample was unrepresentative;[2] but recently, the sociologist Peter Rossi obtained similar results with a more representative group.[3] Rossi showed those questioned a list of 140 offenses, described fairly specifically (e.g., "breaking and entering a house and stealing a radio"), and asked them to rate the "seriousness" of each offense from 1 to 9 in ascending order of gravity. A substantial degree of consen-

---

* See Chapter 4. Moreover, considerations other than seriousness enter, to an unknown degree, into the determination of statutory maxima. If the legislature sets the maximum prison term for selling narcotics above that for assault with a weapon, one often cannot tell whether that is because it regarded the narcotics offense as the more serious, or felt an exceptional punishment was necessary to deter such offenses, or wished simply to keep narcotics dealers off the streets longer.

sus was found in the ranking of the crimes; and there was comparatively little variation in response among different racial, occupational, and educational subgroups. The researchers noted:

> In asking the respondent to rate crimes, we did not specify what was "seriousness." Nor did we ask respondents what they meant by their ratings. Obviously, respondents imparted some meaning to the term, a meaning shared sufficiently by others to produce [this high] degree of consensus. . . .
>
> [T]he norms defining how serious various criminal acts are considered to be, are quite widely distributed among blacks and whites, males and females, high and low socio-economic levels, and among levels of educational attainment.[4]

Whatever the complexities in the concept of seriousness, such studies suggest that people from widely different walks of life can make common-sense judgments on the comparative gravity of offenses and come to fairly similar conclusions.

ANALYTICALLY, seriousness has two major components: *harm* and *culpability*.

The seriousness of an offense depends, in the first instance, on how harmful the conduct is: that is, on the degree of injury caused or risked. (To cite an elementary example, armed robbery is more serious than a burglary, because the threatened harm is so much greater.)

An offense ought not be deemed serious unless the harm is grave. Among common victimizing crimes, for example, only those are serious which produce or threaten devastating consequences to the victim: inconvenience to the victim (even substantial inconvenience) should not be enough.

In assessing harmfulness, the emphasis should be on the harm *characteristically* done or risked by an offense of that kind. This emphasis on harm in the typical case is necessary, as we shall elaborate later, in order to control discretion and to assure that the severity of penalties is knowable in advance.

The other major component of seriousness is the degree of the offender's culpability: that is, the degree to which he may justly be held to blame for the consequences or risks of his act.° Here there is one well-established principle: that prohibited behavior causing (or risking) the same harm varies in seriousness depending on whether it is intentional, reckless, negligent, or punishable regardless of the actor's intent ("strict liability"); these distinctions usually are recognized in statutory definitions of crimes. But there are other factors bearing on the degree of culpability, such as (1) the extent to which the act was precipitated by the victim's own misconduct; and (2) whether (if the crime involved several persons) the defendant was a central or only a peripheral participant.

Culpability, in turn, affects the assessment of harm. In gauging seriousness, one should ordinarily look to the harm characteristically done or risked by the act of a *single* offender, rather than the totality of damage caused by

° Culpability, it should be noted, affects both questions of liability ("Should the person be punished at all?") and questions of allocation ("How severely should he be punished?"). Liability is the threshold question: whether the behavior involved sufficient culpability to be punishable at all. (In some jurisdictions, for example, the infliction of physical injury short of death is not punishable unless done intentionally or recklessly: negligence is not sufficient for criminal liability.) But once that threshold has been passed, the question of degree of culpability still has to be considered in deciding the seriousness of the offense. (It has to be decided, for example, how much more serious intentionally inflicted harm is than recklessly inflicted harm.)

behavior of that kind. (Shoplifting is a minor crime because
the harm done by a single act of shoplifting is relatively
trivial, although the total economic harm done by all acts of
shoplifting may well be substantial.) This focus on the single
act is based on notions of culpability: the individual may be
held responsible for the risks or consequences of his own
acts, but not for the cumulated damage done by others who
happen to commit the same crime, since he has no control
over their actions.*

There are a number of complications involved in the
concepts of harm and culpability. One is: harm to what
interests? Different crimes may not be readily comparable
in harmfulness, because the interests affected are dissimilar.† Another question concerns risk of harm. How likely
must the risk be? With respect to conduct that risks a given
degree of harm, should it matter whether or not the injury
actually occurs? Some issues concerning culpability will also
prove troublesome—for instance, the question of the offender's motives. (Should it, for example, be a mitigating
circumstance that the offender was motivated by a desire to
help someone, or that he sincerely believed the law he
violated to be wrong?) Finally, there is the matter of whose

---

* Some conduct (e.g., an environmental offense such as littering) is prohibited
primarily because of its aggregate effects, rather than because of the consequences
of a single violation. But even here one should, in assessing the seriousness of a
single violation, discount the aggregate harm in some approximate way to reflect
the fact that *this* offender's contribution to the harm was minuscule.

† For instance: if someone steals a car, a valuable item of property is lost; if he
breaks into a home and steals a TV set, the property loss is less but the occupant's
privacy (and sense of physical security) is infringed. To determine which crime is
the more serious, one therefore has to decide the relative importance of these
interests. Common-sense judgments of seriousness appear to be guided by some
informal sense of priorities of interests: most people would regard the burglary as
more serious than the car theft and, if asked why, would say that a person's safety
and privacy is more important than his belongings.

standards should govern. To what extent ought the governmental body charged with setting sentencing standards make its own assessments of seriousness? To what extent must it adhere to the community's perceptions of seriousness, as reflected in surveys such as Rossi's? ° (How this last question should be resolved would depend, in part, on one's theory of government—on how much one thinks officials should be permitted to rely on their own judgments rather than on popular preferences on particular issues.)

Yet, despite these complexities, we do not expect insuperable difficulties in developing a workable ranking of seriousness. Difficulty in grading offenses will occur mainly when making comparisons *across* major genera of crimes. (Familiar crimes such as burglary, robbery, and assault have enough in common to facilitate judging their comparative gravity; the problem arises when offenses are markedly dissimilar—e.g., how does bribery rank against burglary?) It also should be emphasized that we are speaking of only a few gradations of seriousness. While refined discriminations in relative gravity would undoubtedly be hard to make, it

° Certainly, the criteria for seriousness will have to be distilled from the basic norms of conduct of this society. For the standard-setting agency is not deciding in a cultural vacuum: it is deciding seriousness for a system of penalties designed for this culture with its particular moral traditions. But the question remains: Must the criteria for seriousness reflect community attitudes *in detail?* If survey research shows that most people regard a particular offense as very serious, is the standard-setting agency obliged to reflect that view in classifying its gravity? Or may that agency question the popular view if, for example, it seems to it to be based on misconceptions about the amount of harm involved?

It is worth mentioning that this problem of whose standards is not unique to our theory of allocating penalties. Suppose, instead, that the state were to allocate penalties according to a theory of predictive restraint. It would then have to decide at what point the harm to be prevented becomes important enough to justify confining the individual—and that likewise raises the question: Important enough by whose standards?

should be simpler to devise criteria capable of distinguishing, say, among five or six major degrees of seriousness. For reasons which we shall elaborate in Chapter 16, a small number of gradations may be all that is required in order to construct a workable penalty scale.

10

Prior Criminal Record

THE SERIOUSNESS of "the offense," to which the commensurate-deserts principle looks, embraces the defendant's prior criminal record: the number of his previous convictions and the seriousness of the crimes involved. A first offense, in our view, is deserving of less punishment than a second or third.

In the American criminal justice system, and in most others with which we are familiar, an offender's record of previous convictions considerably influences the severity with which he is punished. The first offender can expect more lenient treatment than the repeater. But why so?

Grounds other than commensurate deserts could account for this practice. One theory is predictive: the more often someone has offended in the past, the more likely he is to do it again—and hence, arguably, the greater reason for restraining him. Another theory has to do with deterrence:

having continued to commit crimes despite previous punish-ments, repeaters might as a class require a greater penalty to induce them to desist. But such explanations would not suffice, given the preeminence we have accorded commen-surate deserts. Unless the repeater *deserves* it,* he could not, in our theory, be punished any differently from the first offender.[1]

The reason for treating the first offense as less serious is, we think, that repetition alters the degree of culpability that may be ascribed to the offender. In assessing a first offender's culpability, it ought to be borne in mind that he was, at the time he committed the crime, only one of a large audience to whom the law impersonally addressed its prohibitions. His first conviction, however, should call dramatically and personally to his attention that the behav-ior is condemned. A repetition of the offense following that conviction may be regarded as more culpable, since he persisted in the behavior after having been forcefully censured for it through his prior punishment.

Our view of the first infraction as less culpable is reinforced when the evidentiary problems confronting the sentencer are considered. With an instrument as crude as the fact-finding process of the criminal law, the degree of culpability of the defendant is a judgment in which one seldom can have great confidence in any single instance.

---

* The idea that repetition alters what the actor deserves is by no means limited to the criminal law. Consistency is an important consideration in judging someone's deserts in any context. Consistently good performance is seen as meriting more commendation; consistently bad, more blame. Winning a series of races entitles the successful competitor to a special prize, such as the right to retire the trophy. According this greater recognition is not a forecast that he will win future races, for the hazards of prediction in such competitive enterprises are well known: it is recognition that a string of victories is the greater achievement.

Did the defendant really intend the harm (or was intent merely imputed to him because the criminal law presumes persons to intend the natural and probable consequences of their acts)? Was there any contributory fault on the part of the victim? If the crime implicated several persons, was the defendant a central or only a peripheral participant? It is hard to be certain in a single situation, but with each repetition, the ascription of culpability can be made with a little more confidence. That the offender could have been provoked, for example, is ordinarily less believable on the third occasion he assaults someone than on the first.°

Our view of repetition has an important collateral advantage of parsimony in inflicting pain. Penalties for first offenses can be kept on the low side, reflecting the doubts just mentioned about the extent of the offender's culpability. More severe penalties would be reserved mainly for offenders who had offended and been punished before. A salient feature of the penalty scale we will be proposing is a substantial cutting back of penalties for first offenses.

In taking this view of a prior criminal record, we wish to emphasize that even a second or third offense ought not be deemed serious unless the harm done or risked by that offense was great. Repetition affects one of the components

---

° This idea—of repetition as permitting the sentencer to ascribe culpability with greater confidence—loses some of its force if the current offense is sufficiently dissimilar from the prior ones. It suffices for our purposes, however, if repetition usually (although not always) permits a more confident ascription of culpability— since norms of seriousness under our scheme are to be based chiefly on the typical case. As will be more fully explained in Chapter 12, standard penalties will be established that are lower for first offenses than for second or third violations; and some discretionary variation from the standard penalties will be permitted for special circumstances of aggravation or mitigation. The power to mitigate could then be invoked in those special situations where repetition does not appear to have its usual bearing on the offender's culpability.

of seriousness—culpability—but the other component, the harmfulness of the conduct, is more important still. Repetition of an offense that does comparatively little harm cannot justly be made the occasion for severe punishment, as is true under multiple-offender statutes in force in many states today.° [2]

How much time has passed since the previous conviction should also be taken into account. The greater the time between the preceding offense and the current one, the harder it becomes to argue that the prior offense bears on the ascription of culpability for the current one. Provision should be made for "decay" of the offenders' criminal record, with convictions in the distant past being disregarded.

Since a record of prior offenses bears both on the offender's deserts and on the likelihood of recidivism, what practical difference does it make which theory is adopted? The difference is this. The commensurate-deserts principle looks only to the seriousness of the offender's prior crimes. A theory of predictive restraint, by contrast, allows one to consider not only his criminal record but *anything else* that bears on his likelihood of offending again: matters of the offender's social status having nothing to do with his blameworthiness—e.g., his lack of a fixed abode, a steady job, or a high school diploma—could warrant a longer sentence to the extent that they indicated a higher statistical likelihood of recidivism. It is this attention to matters of status that we find objectionable. Perhaps jobless offenders are, on average, more likely to recidivate than those with

° Multiple-offender statutes typically impose long prison terms—sometimes as much as life imprisonment—upon the third conviction for *any* felony. (The law of some jurisdictions defines any theft over $100 as a felony.)

steady jobs; but it is still offensive to punish a criminal more severely, irrespective of the gravity of the crimes he has perpetrated, on the grounds that he happens to have no job. The commensurate-deserts principle, while taking prior crimes into account, would exclude these other factors.

The U.S. Parole Board's criteria for parole release are a case in point.[3] While the board looks mainly to the seriousness of the inmate's most recent offense, it also considers his likelihood of recidivism as indicated on a predictive index. Although several of the factors used in the predictive index concern his prior criminal record, some do not: the offender is scored on whether he has completed high school; whether he has been employed; and whether he has a spouse or children with whom he plans to live. In our theory, these last factors would be ruled out: we would look only to the number and seriousness of prior convictions. As it happens, that information would also have considerable predictive power—because subsequent criminality shows a substantial degree of correlation with prior criminal record.[4] But the disposition then depends only on matters that were within the offender's control (his criminal behavior) and not on matters of social status that may have been largely beyond his power to alter.

11

Severity of Punishments

SEVERITY REFERS to how unpleasant the punishment is. It should be judged in the light of general tolerances for suffering in the society: punishment is only one kind of unpleasantness people may experience, and it should be assessed by comparison with other sufferings they might encounter. If, when thus judged, a punishment is very painful, it qualifies as severe. (The severity of a punishment thus ought not be gauged merely by its place on a scale of penalties: were a punishment to rank low on a penalty scale but nevertheless be very painful by comparison with other commonplace misfortunes, it is still severe.)

The assessment of severity, as the assessment of the harmfulness of the offense, should be standardized: the focus should be on how unpleasant the punishment *characteristically* is. Such standardization is necessary as a limit on discretion, as we shall argue in the next chapter. It is also needed as a safeguard against class justice. Judges sometimes impose different penalties on persons convicted of similar crimes, in the hope of producing equivalent amounts of discomfort: the middle-class person is put on probation and the ghetto youth jailed for the same infraction, on the theory that the former's sensitivities are greater. More drastic measures thus come to be imposed chiefly on those of lower status who are deemed to have "less to lose"—but only because they have lost so much already through their deprived social situation.

The principle of commensurate deserts calls for maintenance of a "proportion" between the seriousness of the crime and the severity of the penalty. That leaves the question of how the "proportion" is to be judged. There is a rough intuitive sense of what is plainly *dis*proportionate: imprisonment is "too much" for petty theft, a warning "too little" for mayhem. Such extremes aside, however, intuition does not give sufficient guidance, and it is necessary to seek principles for matching offenses with their deserved penalties.

There are two distinct concerns: (1) the *internal composition* of the scale—how offenses are to be punished relative to each other; and (2) the *magnitude* of the scale—what the scale's overall dimensions should be. The principle of commensurate deserts controls the internal composition of the scale, but, as we shall see, places only approximate outside limits on its magnitude.

Internal Composition of the Scale. The principle of commensurate deserts imposes, in the first place, an ordering on penalties. Punishments are to be arranged so that their relative painfulness corresponds with the comparative seriousness of offenses. Spacing is likewise important: penalties ought not, for example, to be crowded together so closely as to obscure distinctions in seriousness among offenses. The principle also requires that infractions of equal seriousness be punished with equal severity. For a given category of offense, therefore, a specific penalty level should be set that is applicable to all instances, except when special aggravating or mitigating circumstances can be shown to have existed.

These requirements restrict the extent to which the scale may be varied internally for purposes unrelated to offenders' deserts. Raising the penalty for one kind of offense to achieve more deterrence will throw the ranking of offenses out of kilter, unless all other penalties are adjusted accordingly. Holding one individual offender longer than others convicted of the same crime, in order to incapacitate him, will violate the equality requirement.

Magnitude of the Scale. The principle of commensurate deserts imposes some outside limits—albeit fuzzy ones—on the whole scale's magnitude.

Commensurate deserts restricts severe punishments to serious crimes. The penalty scale ought not be inflated so much that non-serious crimes also receive severe penalties (severe, that is, in our previously defined sense of being very unpleasant, given the prevailing tolerances for suffering). Severe punishments for non-serious offenses overstate blame: the offender is being treated as more reprehensible than the harmfulness of his acts (and the extent of his culpability) justify. This objection holds even if the whole scale has been elevated so much that the penalty ranks low in comparative harshness alongside other penalties. Irrespective of other penalties, when an offender has been visited with much suffering, the implicit condemnation is great. Punishing someone with several years' imprisonment —once the painfulness of that sanction is understood—connotes that he must be very reprehensible to deserve *that*; and if other transgressors are made to suffer more, that only implies that they are still more blameworthy.°

Imprecise as this limitation on severe punishment is, it has some practical usefulness. Consider the sanction of incarceration, which (for reasons to be spelled out later) we regard as a severe punishment. Assuming it is severe, our principle limits its use (if it is used at all) to offenses that qualify as serious; and, as we noted earlier, an offense should not be deemed serious unless the harm it does (or risks) is great. Harm is admittedly a debatable matter; but, at least, when someone proposes that certain classes of offenses be punishable by incarceration, the burden rests on him to show why those offenses do or threaten sufficient injury to be judged serious. That changes the character of the debate: a prison sentence for such crimes cannot be justified merely on the grounds that worse offenses are punished more severely still.

But do all serious offenses require severe punishments? Not necessarily. The penalty structure could be scaled down so as to inflict less-than-severe punishments for offenses in

---

° Another reason for restricting severe punishments to serious crimes concerns the character of people's scruples about unlawful conduct. Drastic measures ought to be employed only against behavior which is so reprehensible that, the threat of legal penalties aside, most people could be expected to have the strongest moral inhibitions against it. It is not enough that the behavior be properly classified as criminal and that there be ample notice of the consequences of violation—for, given human impulsiveness, people still will too easily resort to behavior that does not seem to them particularly evil. Were the entire scale inflated so much that non-serious offenses received severe punishments, violators could suffer devastating consequences for conduct which, to the moral judgment of the ordinary person, seemed only venially wrong.

the lower range of those that are serious. For sentencers' judgments of offenders' deserts will perforce be rather crude: e.g., such judgments will have to be made mainly by reference to the typical case, overlooking significant differences among individual transgressions. Such a scaling-down would be one way of recognizing how fallible decisions about offenders' deserts are.

There is a lower limit, however, albeit an imprecise one. Severe penalties should be required for the most serious offenses, such as the intentional and unprovoked infliction of grievous bodily injury. No less would express the requisite condemnation of the conduct.

These desert-based limits leave considerable choice as to the magnitude of the scale. To the extent the deserts principle leaves choice, deterrence may then be taken into account.° Consider a system which used imprisonment as the penalty only for serious offenses, and suppose the question is whether the scale should run up to a maximum prison term of five years or ten. Either maximum would be consistent with the limit of commensurateness just described: the penalties in question are severe, but this would be permissible since the offenses are serious. It therefore becomes appropriate to consider how much more deterrent effect, overall, an up-to-ten-year scale is likely to have than an up-to-five-year scale. Unless the ten-year scale was expected to have substantially greater deterrent effect, the lower magnitude would be preferred. (We are, it should be stressed, comparing magnitudes and looking to their overall

° Where the pursuit of deterrence conflicts with the principle of commensurate deserts, the latter principle should have priority. But where the principle is indifferent as between two possible magnitudes, as we argue is the case here, one becomes entitled to opt for the one that has the greater deterrent usefulness.

deterrent effect—not deciding the punishment for a particular species of offense by its deterrent effect. A particular offense would be ranked on the scale according to its seriousness, once the scale's magnitude had been decided.)

It may be possible to delineate the limits on magnitude better than we have done, but the foregoing should suffice to illustrate the basic idea: in deciding the magnitude of the scale, deterrence may be considered within whatever leeway remains after the outer bounds set by commensurate deserts have been established. Once a scale of a certain magnitude has been chosen, however, the internal composition of the scale should be determined by the principle of commensurate deserts.

IV

Toward a
Sentencing System

UsING the conceptions just set forth, we ought to be able to sketch the outlines of a sentencing system. The theory should give guidance as to how much discretion officials should have in deciding the disposition of convicted offenders, and what kinds of penalties should be prescribed.

12

Discretion and Sentencing Standards

WIDE DISCRETION in sentencing has been sustained by the traditional assumptions about rehabilitation and predictive restraint. Once these assumptions are abandoned, the basis for such broad discretion crumbles. On our theory, the sentence is not a means of altering the offender's behavior that has to be especially suited to his "needs"; it is a deserved penalty based on the seriousness of his past criminal conduct. In order for the principle of commensurate deserts to govern, there *must* be standards specifying how much offenders receive for different crimes. Were questions of offenders' deserts left mainly to the discretion of individual judges, no consistent scale of penalties would emerge: one judge could treat certain offenses as serious and punish accordingly; another judge, having a different set of values, could deal with the same infractions as minor ones.

Without sentencing standards, moreover, there would be little to prevent the individual judge from making decisions on grounds other than commensurate deserts (e.g., basing his sentences on predictions of dangerousness if that was the sentencing theory he preferred).

General guidelines are suited for defining the comparative gravity of different categories of crimes and specifying the punishments which ordinarily apply to them. Some degree of flexibility is needed, however, to deal with the atypical cases—where the harmfulness of the particular offender's conduct or the extent of his culpability is substantially greater or less than is characteristic for that kind of offense.

We therefore suggest that each crime category be assigned a "presumptive sentence"—that is, a specific penalty based on the crime's characteristic seriousness. This would be the disposition for most offenders convicted of that crime. However, the judge should be authorized—within specified limits—to depart from the presumptive sentence if he finds aggravating or mitigating circumstances. Uniform treatment is thus provided for the unexceptional cases that make up the bulk of judges' caseloads, while still allowing variation in out-of-the-ordinary cases. (This would be a significant departure from the pattern of current sentencing statutes, where no specific penalty is fixed as the presumptive sentence and only outside limits—usually maxima, occasionally maxima and minima—are set.)

Using this approach, the sentencing system should have the following structure:

• Graded levels of seriousness would be established, and the guidelines would specify which offense categories belong on which seriousness levels.

• For each level of seriousness, a specific penalty—the presumptive sentence—would be prescribed. An offender convicted of a crime of that gradation of seriousness would ordinarily receive this sentence.

• For those offenders who had been convicted before, there would be a prescribed increase in the presumptive sentence, depending on the number and seriousness of the prior crimes.

• The judge would have authority to raise the penalty above or reduce it below the presumptive sentence, in cases where he finds there were special circumstances affecting the gravity of the violation° and where he specifies what these circumstances of aggravation or mitigation were. But such variations could not depart from the presumptive sentence by more than a prescribed amount. The limits on the permitted variations should be designed to preserve the basic ranking of penalties—and restrict overlaps in the severity of punishments for offenses of characteristically distinct seriousness. Intentional homicides, even under mitigating circumstances, should preserve their rank above, say, burglaries.

• General principles governing aggravation and mitigation should be set forth in the standards.† In our theory, only

° That is, if he found that either the harmfulness of the particular offender's conduct or the degree of his culpability was greater or less than usual for that kind of crime. In an assault, for example, it could be an aggravating factor that the physical injury was more than usually severe (increased harm); and a mitigating factor that the act was done in response to provocation by the victim (reduced culpability).

† A statement of principles governing aggravation and mitigation would be preferable, we think, to a mere listing of aggravating and mitigating factors such as some European codes contain. (For a description of some such European codes, see G. O. W. Mueller and Fré Le Poole, "Appellate Review of Legal But Excessive Sentence: A Comparative Study," 21 *Vanderbilt L. Rev.* 411 [1968].)

those special circumstances that affect the seriousness of the offender's crime could qualify.

To illustrate: Suppose a defendant were convicted of armed robbery for the second time. Were no special circumstances of aggravation or mitigation shown, he would receive the disposition which the guidelines specify as the presumptive sentence for a second armed robbery. Were there several participants in the robbery and his role in the crime a peripheral one, however, this could be a mitigating circumstance permitting a limited reduction below the presumptive sentence.

This scheme could be altered with experience. The number of gradations of seriousness could be increased or decreased, or the range of permitted variation widened or narrowed.

Any scheme—with more discretion or less—will lead to some inequities. Standards will operate arbitrarily in some instances, just as discretion risks disparities and bias. The most one can do is find a reasonable mix—to allow some degree of discretion structured by standards. Because our proposal would limit the permitted variation from the presumptive sentence, there will be some cases that fit badly—where the maximum permissible punishment seems too low, or the minimum permissible too high. We recognize this as a disadvantage, but we feel that the alternative of not having such limits would have worse consequences still.

INDETERMINACY of sentence has been another outgrowth of the conventional assumptions: the timing of the offender's release, it was thought, should depend on his progress toward cure and the degree of continuing risk he represents. Our theory undercuts the need for indeterminacy. The commensurate-deserts principle looks to the past—to the seriousness of the defendant's crimes. Seriousness—the extent of the harm done or risked and the degree of the actor's culpability—can just as well be ascertained at the time of conviction as at an indefinite later date: for this purpose, as Marvin Frankel states, "whatever complexities and imponderables there are—and there are plenty . . . there is none that is not knowable on the day of sentencing." * 1

The elimination of indeterminacy should be a welcome change to convicted offenders—who now suffer the agonies of not knowing how long their punishments will continue. When indeterminacy is eliminated, however, sentences will have to be scaled down. Many judges now impose long sentences in the expectation (not always fulfilled) that a parole board will permit earlier release. Under our approach, the initially imposed sentence would be the one actually served.

IT IS sometimes supposed that the only alternative to wide sentencing discretion is to have *legislatures* set the sentencing standards. Suggestions to limit discretion evoke argu-

---

* An alternative, suggested by Norval Morris, is to have the final decision as to the amount of punishment (for serious offenses, at least) set a few weeks after the initial sentence. "The judge," Morris states, "imposes sentence at a time of high emotional response to the facts of the crime. Even within our grossly dilatory system of justice, the sentence follows closely upon the public narration of the criminal events, if not upon the commission of the crime." The delay would enable the decision to be made "in what one hopes will be a less punitive social atmosphere." However, this would not require indeterminacy. The decision still could be made at a *determinate* time knowable in advance and set fairly soon after conviction.

ments that legislative bodies are ill suited for that purpose. Historically, legislatures have shown little inclination to deal with controversial sentencing issues, preferring to leave them to courts and parole boards. On the relatively infrequent occasions when legislatures have prescribed minimum sentences, these have tended to be extremely harsh.[2] Legislative bodies, the critic of legislatively set sentences could argue, are concerned mainly with the majority of their constituents—and lack the requisite concern with the rights of the minority who are being punished.

The legislature, however, is not the only agency that might set standards for sentencing. The task (including the setting of presumptive sentences) could be performed by the courts. In most American jurisdictions, appellate courts do not review sentences; but were appellate review instituted, as many authorities have urged, the standards could be articulated through case law.[3] Alternatively, the formulation of standards could be undertaken by the trial court. (A trial court could—either by consultation among its members or by establishing a standard-setting panel—prescribe tentative guidelines for disposition, which individual judges would be expected to apply in their sentencing decisions.[*][4] Review of sentences might then permit the appellate court to affirm or modify these guidelines.) Courts, arguably, are suited for this standard-setting role because they have historically performed the sentencing function and have been accustomed to dealing with issues where the majority's interests in crime control must be weighed against the rights of individuals facing punishment. Another alternative is to

---

[*] A research project under the direction of Leslie Wilkins and Don Gottfredson is now exploring the feasibility of judicially developed sentencing guidelines in two state jurisdictions.

have an administrative agency prescribe the standards, as
the U.S. Board of Parole and the California parole board
have done in promulgating guidelines for parole release.[5]
Hybrid solutions are also possible. For example, standards
could be set by a special rule-making agency established
under the aegis of the courts.[6]

While some of us feel it preferable for the courts to
formulate the standards, the decision depends, ultimately,
on one's theory of government—on who one thinks should
be entrusted with setting public policy in a democratic
society. In practice, it could also depend on the staffing and
competence of different agencies within a given jurisdiction.
The main point is that there is a choice: the decision to have
sentencing norms does not compel the selection of a
particular agency to set them.

IT HAS BEEN ESTIMATED that some ninety percent of
criminal cases are plea-bargained: the prosecutor negotiates
a charge reduction in exchange for a guilty plea. While
some believe that the overburdened court system would
cease functioning altogether if all cases were brought to
trial, the abuses of plea-bargaining have become notorious.[7]
Various proposals for reform have been put forward,
ranging from abolition of plea-bargaining[8] to increased
judicial supervision of the bargaining process.[9]

Plea negotiation, as practiced, has given excessive bargaining leverage to the prosecution. Here sentencing standards of the kind we suggest could be of some help. In part,
the prosecutor's bargaining power comes from the defendant's knowledge that if he does not agree to plead guilty to a
reduced charge the prosecution may have sufficient evi-

dence to convict on the more severely punishable original charge—and this element of prosecutorial leverage would remain under our proposal. However, the existing system gives the prosecutor undue added bargaining leverage through the threat of exemplary severity if the defendant refuses to plead guilty. The defendant who insists on going to trial not only risks conviction on the more serious original charge but incurs the extra risk that, if convicted, he will be made to suffer a punishment that is uncharacteristically severe for that charge. Our suggested sentencing standards would reduce that threat by limiting the court's discretion. If the defendant refuses to bargain and is convicted on the original charge, he would get the sentence for it prescribed under the rules. Exemplary punishments could not so easily be handed out to those who insisted on their right to trial, and the defendant would have a better idea of the penalty he might expect if he were to lose his case.*

A second major problem associated with plea-bargaining is the absence of standards governing the prosecutor's bargaining decisions. In deciding what bargain to offer, the

---

* While our suggested scheme allows some discretionary upward variation from the presumptive sentence, that could not so readily be used to penalize defendants who refused to plead guilty. The rules should specify that refusal to plead guilty is not an aggravating factor, as it does not bear on the seriousness of the offense. And limits would be placed on the amount of upward variation allowed on *any* ground.

The prosecutor could try to compensate for the bargaining leverage he loses under our scheme by starting his bargaining with a higher charge. But, on a given state of the evidence, the higher the charge, the more difficult it becomes for the prosecution to prove its case in court, and hence the less credible the threat.

It would also be necessary, however, to limit other methods of inflicting exemplary penalties on those who refuse to plead guilty—such as resort to consecutive sentences. (A criminal act usually constitutes a violation of several provisions of the criminal law. There now exists discretion to inflate penalties by imposing consecutive sentences for multiple violations involved in a single criminal transaction.)

prosecutor is not required to abide by any set of principles
—so different prosecutors are able to decide differently,
with glaring disparities resulting. The adoption of standards
governing judges' sentencing decisions still could leave the
prosecutor free to bargain on whatever basis he chose. To
overcome this difficulty, either plea-bargaining must be
abolished or it must be subjected to much closer controls,
designed to maintain a reasonable degree of consistency
between the prosecution's bargaining decisions and the
standards for sentencing.[10] Deciding which of these alternatives, abolition or regulation, is preferable and how either
might be implemented requires an inquiry beyond this
book's scope—namely, a full examination of the role of
prosecutorial discretion. (The problem of how to limit
plea-bargaining discretion, we should note, is not unique to
our theory but inheres in any theory that advocates that
sentencing be governed by a consistent set of standards.)

13

Incarceration

WE TURN to the measure which prompted our inquiry in the first place—incarceration. We recommend stringent limitations of its use.

As PRISONS acquire a bad name, there is a tendency to switch labels: offenders continue to be confined, but in places no longer called prisons. To avoid confusing name with substance, a general definition of incarceration is necessary.

We define incarceration as *collective residential restraint*.

By *restraint* we mean that the individual is restricted to a narrowly circumscribed place. He is put there without regard to his wishes and cannot leave without permission. The place may have high walls but does not have to: if he is prohibited from leaving and subject to penalties if he does, he is restrained.

By *residential* we mean that the place is, for a specified period, the individual's principal abode—most of his nights and a substantial portion of his waking hours must be spent there. A free person, Erving Goffman has pointed out, "tends to sleep, play, and work in different places, with different co-participants, under different authorities." [1] An incarcerated person must perform most or all of these activities in the same place and under the same authority. That place and those in charge of it, therefore, largely determine his activities and the quality of his life.

By *collective* we mean that the person must live in the immediate company of others, not members of his family or persons of his own choosing.*

Traditional penal institutions—jails and prisons—obviously fall within this definition. So do many purported "alternatives" to imprisonment such as enforced residence in a halfway house, "adult boarding home," † [2] or the like. Whether the place of confinement has a dozen residents or a thousand—whether it is a brownstone in town or a fortress in a remote rural location—is immaterial to our definition.

---

* Solitary confinement is not collective but is usually an adjunct to collective restraint.

† The National Council on Crime and Delinquency, in a recent policy statement entitled "The Nondangerous Offender Should Not Be Imprisoned," has recommended the use of "adult boarding homes" as an alternative to imprisonment. In the Council's words: ". . . superior to imprisonment in every respect, is the adult boarding home (patterned on the foster home for the placement of juvenile delinquents), a residence for a small number of offenders, supervised by correctional personnel or volunteers." On our definition, this would be merely another species of incarceration.

Similarly, the Model Penal Code authorizes a judge to use probation to incarcerate: the judge may, as a condition of probation, require the defendant "to . . . reside in a facility established for the . . . residence of persons on probation."

One type of institution may be preferable to another: small size may reduce the need for regimentation, and location in the community may allow for easier access. But these differences should not cause one to overlook the common incarcerative nature of such places.

Excluded from our definition are modes of restraint which are not collective and residential. A person compelled to attend a designated place during portions of his leisure time is not incarcerated, if he continues to live at home and be at liberty most of the time. (Later we shall propose such non-residential restriction of free time as an alternative to incarceration.)

Insane asylums, juvenile reformatories, and institutions for the mentally retarded also entail collective residential restraint. However, our concern is with incarceration when it is used to punish convicted adults.

INCARCERATION is a severe penalty, even in the "nicest" places of confinement—with smaller size, better location, improved services, and less regimentation than is customary in American prisons today. The loss of liberty is itself a great deprivation. And confinement works a dramatic change in the quality of the person's existence: he can no longer see whom he would like to see, or continue the pursuits important in his life. With this loss of autonomy, there comes a sense of being cut off from all that makes living worthwhile. In Erving Goffman's words:

> . . . among inmates in many total institutions there is a strong feeling that time spent in the establishment is time wasted or destroyed or taken from one's life; it is time that must be written off; it is something that must be "done" or "marked" or

"put in" or "pulled." In prisons and mental hospitals, a general statement of how well one is adapting to the institution may be phrased in terms of how one is doing time, whether easily or hard. This time is something its doers have bracketed off for constant conscious consideration in a way not quite found on the outside. As a result, the inmate tends to feel that for the duration of his required stay—his sentence—he has been totally exiled from living.[3]

Compounding the loss of liberty is enforced intimacy with uncongenial strangers. Inmates who are forcibly kept together may have or can develop strong antagonisms based on race, social class, ideology, gang conflict, or personal animosity: close living aggravates such tensions. As one ex-inmate put it: "I have nearly forgotten all about Penton-ville, now, but I think one of the worse memories of my stay was to be forced upon people's company I hated." [4]

The symbolism of being incarcerated compounds its pains: it is not pleasant to live where the very walls are a reminder that one has been singled out as a miscreant.

These pains of confinement can perhaps be alleviated somewhat by allowing inmates to leave for specified inter-vals to work or visit friends and family. But incarceration is severe even under such circumstances, since the person still must spend most of his time cut off from the pursuits and companions of his choice.

ONE THING is clear under our theory: incarceration, being a severe punishment, must never be used except for that narrow range of offenses that qualify as serious. But should it be retained even for serious crimes? When we began our study, we doubted that it should, given what we knew about conditions in American prisons. But, ultimately, we did not choose abolition—at least for now.

The principle of commensurate deserts, as noted earlier, requires severe penalties for serious crimes. One therefore has these limited options: keep incarceration or fashion a severe penalty of another kind. Given that choice, we opt for incarceration.

One reason for preferring incarceration is simply that we have not found another satisfactory severe punishment. Historically, the alternative was corporal punishment, but that is worse. Incarceration at least can be divided into weeks, months, and years—and its duration prescribed by standards. Given the numerous possibilities that modern technology affords for inflicting pain and the difficulty of measuring degrees of subjective distress, effectively controlling the use of corporal punishment is virtually an impossible task.* Exile is another possibility, having the advantage that the offender can move to the place of exile with his family, rather than having to live with strangers; but it presents problems about which we still feel we know too little.† House arrest, used in some countries for political prisoners, likewise allows the person to live with his family;

---

* Beyond the question of effective control, corporal punishment poses disturbing ethical problems. Besides any physical pain involved, intentional corporal maltreatment evokes in its victim intense feelings of humiliation and terror. (That is a reason why crimes of violence are regarded as so serious, even when substantial bodily injury does not ensue.) Ought a civilized state ever to visit such mortifications? Might there not exist a right to the integrity of one's own body, that not even the state's interests in punishing may override?

† One problem is: exile to where? Were the offender merely barred from his customary residence but given a wide choice of where else to live, the penalty could lack the requisite severity. On the other hand, exile to a small territory where offenders must live in close proximity with one another comes close to the collective residential restraint which characterizes incarceration.

but it has the weakness of class bias in a society such as ours: affluent offenders could live comfortably in their suburban homes, while poor offenders could not escape their tenement flats. Perhaps, with sufficient ingenuity, other methods could be devised—but we feel that caution should be exercised: with severe sanctions, there is danger that any novel alternative would prove still more painful and more susceptible of abuse than incarceration.

A further reason for choosing incarceration is its incapacitative effect: those confined cannot commit offenses against persons on the outside.* This reliance on incapacitation does not violate our principles (as predictive restraint would),† for we are not proposing to depart from the severity that is deserved. We are speaking, instead, of the choice between incarceration and an *equally severe* hypothetical penalty (assuming one could be devised), so that the commensurate-deserts principle would be satisfied by either disposition. We are thus entitled to choose incarceration because it incapacitates, without sacrificing our requirement of justice.°°

This incapacitative effect can be achieved, moreover,

---

* But persons inside—other inmates and staff—are not similarly protected. To an unspecified degree, therefore, confinement does not incapacitate so much as shift victimization from persons in the community to persons in the institution.

† For a discussion of why predictive restraint infringes the commensurate-deserts principle, see Chapter 15.

°° Stating this point more generally: a proposed allocation of penalties must, in our theory, first satisfy the requirement of justice—namely, the commensurate-deserts principle. Once that criterion is met, however, one is entitled to prefer one kind of sanction over another on utilitarian grounds.

There is, however, a political risk in relying upon incarceration for its incapacitative usefulness. To the extent this sanction is used to isolate, there may be public demand to widen its use in order to prevent more recidivist crime—making it harder to keep the system's severe punishments within the narrow bounds that the commensurate-deserts principle requires.

without need to rely on predictions of individual dangerousness. Incarceration can be prescribed as the only authorized severe punishment—so that all offenders convicted of sufficiently serious crimes would be confined, irrespective of the likelihood of their returning to crime. As long as this group contains *any* potential recidivists, confining the whole group will prevent some crimes from occurring. And no offender—dangerous or not—would be punished more severely than deserved by his past offense.

We wish to stress, however, that our choice of incarceration is *conditional*. Our arguments for this sanction would no longer stand if a satisfactory alternative severe penalty were devised, and if it was confirmed that incarceration was sufficiently criminogenic.* [5] In the latter event, the incapacitative effects of confinement would be cancelled out by an increase in crimes committed by offenders after their release.

LENGTH OF CONFINEMENT ought to be stringently rationed. David Rothman has pointed out that Americans have been prodigal about time where sentencing is concerned.[6] Our

---

* While many accounts of prisons describe them as schools for crime, that proposition has seldom rigorously been tested—by examining whether the recidivism rates of otherwise like offenders vary with whether and how long they have been confined. Where it has been tested, the results have been mixed—one careful recent study having shown no correlation between duration of confinement and recidivism. While the person in prison is apt to be exposed to others with criminal skills and interests, he is also growing older—and criminal activity tends to diminish with age.

It should also be noted that incarceration could have an incapacitative effect even if confined offenders showed somewhat higher recidivism rates on release—so long as their subsequent recidivism rate was not *so* much higher as to cancel out the preventive effects of having been incarcerated.

highly time-conscious culture—which customarily measures time in seconds, minutes, and hours—measures prison terms in huge dollops: five, ten, fifteen years. Yet time crawls for the incarcerated individual, cut off as he is from pursuits and companions of his choice: a year inside, waiting to get out, seems aeons longer than a year outside, engaged in one's normal activities.[7] Terms of confinement should take this subjectively slower passage of time into account. And it bears repeating: incarceration, even with shorter sentences, should only be invoked against offenders whose crimes are serious.[*] [8]

---

[*] To ensure that incarcerative punishments are restricted to serious offenses, a narrowing of existing discretion to confine accused offenders before trial is also essential. Otherwise, where the offense is not serious enough to deserve a sentence of confinement but the authorities wish to see the person incarcerated anyway, they could simply resort to pretrial detention to accomplish their goal. (Under existing law, a suspect who has been arrested may have to post bail as a condition of release before trial—the ostensible purpose being to ensure his appearance in court. Whether to set bail—and in what amount—is left wholly to the discretion of the individual judge or magistrate. While "excessive bail" is forbidden by the U.S. Constitution, the courts have read this as not precluding the setting of bail beyond the means of the defendant. The bail system has thus become a pretrial detention system in practice, with judges setting bail beyond indigent defendants' means when they are thought likely to abscond or commit other crimes before trial. This discretionary power of pretrial confinement is often used to pressure defendants to accept guilty pleas: unless the accused accepts the bargain offered him by the prosecutor, he risks spending more time in jail before trial than he might if convicted. The power also can be, and has been, used to inflict punishment without trial. The accused is simply held "before trial" for several months, a year, or more and—when he has been thus incarcerated for approximately the period the authorities would have liked to see him serve had he been convicted—the charges against him are dropped and he is released; a formal determination of his guilt or innocence is never made.) To the extent pretrial detention should be retained at all in order to ensure the offender's appearance at trial, judges' discretion to detain should be sharply limited. If, for example, the defendant could be held before trial only if charged with a serious offense and then only for a short period (say, no more than forty-five days), that would restrict (although it would not eliminate) this measure's potential for extracting more stringent penalties than the sentencing rules permit.

THE SEVERITY of incarceration depends not only on its duration but on its conditions. If the rigors of institutional life are stepped up, even a few months' confinement can be made very harsh. We oppose using institutional discipline to add to the severity of confinement. When a staff is given the mission of making life uncomfortable for inmates, it is apt to carry out that mission all too well. Brutality, physical and psychological, is always difficult enough to control in a closed setting: permitting intentionally Spartan regimes compounds the dangers.

We favor minimum interference with confined offenders. The sanction should consist only of the deprivation of the freedom to leave; and the rules governing inmates' behavior within the institution should be limited to those necessary to secure their safe presence. Gradations in severity of incarcerative penalties should be achieved only by varying the *duration* of confinement.

The preference should be for open facilities, without bars or restraining walls. There should also be strict limits on the size of institutions, to reduce the need for regimentation.

Vocational training, education, counseling, and other services should be available to inmates on a voluntary basis. Notwithstanding our earlier-expressed skepticism about mandatory rehabilitation programs,° we strongly favor the provision of *voluntary* services designed to assist offenders with what they regard to be their problems. As the American Friends Service Committee's report, *Struggle for Justice*, has noted, many convicts lack formal education and

---

° It still has to be considered whether mandatory treatment programs should ever be allowed (for the purpose of reducing recidivism rather than helping the offender himself), assuming the programs were to work. We discuss this in Chapter 15.

possess few marketable skills, and some face trying personal difficulties: they could find such services helpful.[9] But we stress that offenders should be free to decide whether or not to participate: if a person is subject to penalties if he refuses to join (or promised more lenient treatment if he does), the program is no longer voluntary.

For the minority of inmates who assault others or try to escape, more secure facilities may be needed. But the decision to transfer prisoners to a secure facility should not be left to the discretion of institutional administrators, as it is today: otherwise, it can become a way of increasing the severity of confinement, for whatever purpose these officials see fit. Instead, there should be guidelines governing transfers. Offenders who are incarcerated should be placed, at first, in an open facility. An inmate should be transferred to a secure facility only if he is found to have committed specified rule infractions involving attempted escape or victimization of others. However, previously confined offenders having a substantial record of assaultive behavior or escape attempts during a previous term of incarceration might be placed directly in the secure facility upon reconviction.*

IN RECOMMENDING the use of incarceration—even to the

---

* Violent or disruptive behavior within the institution would itself be a criminal offense that, if serious enough, should be punishable upon conviction by a prescribed amount of extra confinement.

A more difficult question is whether there should exist power to extend terms administratively for rule infractions. Some of us support a limited "good time" allowance as an incentive for good behavior—permitting a modest percentage (say, 10 percent or 15 percent) of the offender's term to be taken off if he did not commit any major breaches of institutional rules.

limited extent suggested here—we are acutely aware of its dangers. A restricted setting inevitably limits opportunities for outside scrutiny. Inmates' complaints, however legitimate, are apt to be disbelieved simply because the complainants are convicts. Administrators will always be tempted to overlook misconduct by staff, in order to uphold "morale." * Unless inmates are competently and persistently represented; unless the courts are prepared to intervene; and unless the press is willing to expose institutional misconduct, the quality of life in confinement will deteriorate, as it has so often before in the tragic story of the American prison.

* For a description of these dangers, see a recent article by two public-interest lawyers representing prisoners in California, B. E. Bergeson III and William G. Hoerger, "Judicial Misconceptions and the 'Hidden Agenda' in Prisoners' Rights Litigation," 14 *Santa Clara Lawyer* 747 (1974).

14

Alternatives to Incarceration

CURRENT LAW authorizes jail or prison sentences for most criminal offenses, however minor. While the majority of lesser offenders avoid incarceration, an unlucky minority do not: today's prisons and jails are populated not only by murderers and muggers but also by marijuana offenders, prostitutes, pickpockets, writers of bad checks, and car thieves. Under our conception, less severe alternative punishments will have to be devised for the not-so-serious offenses that constitute the bulk of the system's caseload.

While much current reform effort has been devoted to developing alternatives to incarceration, it is often assumed that the offender's rehabilitation is the objective to be attained;[1] and a measure's success or failure is judged by its purported effects on recidivism. In our theory, the alternatives would be conceived of quite differently: as the deliberate infliction of unpleasantness. The degree of the alternatives' unpleasantness should be governed by the principle of commensurate deserts—and thus should range from mild (for minor offenses) to nearly severe (for offenses that rank just below those qualifying for incarceration).

The alternatives should, moreover, be capable of even-handed administration: penalties whose onerousness varies greatly with the degree of zeal of individual officials assigned to carry them out should be avoided where possible. And the alternatives should not interfere with the rights of unconvicted third parties—for it is axiomatic that such persons are entitled to be free from interference by state penal authorities, even if they happen to be related to or associated with someone who is a convicted offender.

Turning to specific measures, we find two particularly suited to our general conception: warning-and-release, and intermittent confinement.

Warning and Unconditional Release. The offender is reproved by the court for his conduct, warned against further criminal acts, and released unconditionally without further supervision.° It is now authorized in some states,² but its use is discretionary with the sentencing judge. We would make it the prescribed penalty for the least serious offenses. While the measure inflicts no material deprivation, it does visit censure: a mild unpleasantness in itself.

Intermittent Confinement. This sanction would require the offender to attend a state-run (or state-designated) facility at specified times outside his regular working hours. It differs from incarceration (in a halfway house, for

---

° The measure differs from the suspended sentence now in use, in that it does not entail any sentence of confinement held in abeyance, which the sentencing court could later impose.

example) in that the restriction is not residential. The offender would continue to live at home, work in the community, and be at liberty during other than the specified hours. It would be the punishment for offenses of intermediate gravity—namely, those too serious for warning-and-release but not serious enough to call for incarceration.* [3]

Intermittent confinement is unpleasant—since it deprives the offender of valued leisure time and forces him to interrupt his regular social life. How unpleasant it is varies with the time taken: the deprivation of every Saturday and Sunday over an extended period is quite stringent; the loss of an occasional evening is considerably milder. If varying amounts of time are prescribed, the penalty can be made commensurate with a wide variety of middle-range offenses. It is, moreover, a penalty that can be applied even-handedly, since everyone has time to lose.† Yet, intermittent confinement is not so painful as incarceration: it does not bring the offender's principal life pursuits to a halt, and close living with uncongenial or hostile strangers is avoided.

There will have to be sanctions to ensure attendance. The penalty for occasional absences could be a warning, coupled perhaps with a requirement that the missed sessions be made up. For continued absences following the warning, the sentence of intermittent confinement could be extended by some stated percentage. For persistent absences there-

---

* A number of West European countries have made extensive use of intermittent confinement, but it has been less frequently practiced here. Where employed, its imposition has largely been a matter of discretion.

† Admittedly, people value time differently and have different amounts of free time available. But time remains an asset more evenly distributed in the population than, say, money.

after, a back-up sanction would have to be prescribed that did not depend on the offender's attendance. If that back-up sanction is more severe (perhaps a brief term of incarceration), most offenders would probably opt for regular attendance in order to avoid it.° And, at least, the choice of the less onerous alternative will have been offered before the severer sanction is invoked.

These measures are punitive in the old-fashioned sense: while less painful than incarceration, their aim is to visit an unpleasantness commensurate with the offense. To some, this may seem too negative an approach. Are alternatives merely to be unpleasant, even if in moderate and carefully graded degrees? Isn't that a wholly unproductive enterprise? Would it not be better if the alternatives were fashioned to provide some positive benefit to the offender or the community? The rehabilitative ideal reflected this understandable desire to do good. And with growing disenchantment with correctional treatment, other variants of this idea are being considered. One is community service, which is now regularly used in Europe[4] and has attracted interest in this country. The offender is to perform work that benefits the public: even if the offender is not thereby reformed, the thinking runs, at least the community gains from the work done. Yet there are dangers in compelling an offender to do good works as punishment. Once criminal sanctions are given a semblance of beneficence, they have a tendency to escalate: if, in punishing, one is (supposedly) doing good, why not do more?

° The theoretical rationale for imposing severer back-up sanctions will be discussed in Chapter 15.

To ILLUSTRATE FURTHER our conception of alternatives, let us briefly consider two that traditionally have been used in this country: fines and probation.

Fines now are authorized for numerous offenses, often in addition to imprisonment. Fines (without imprisonment) are clearly suited to our conception of alternatives. Being deprived of money is unpleasant. Depending on the proportion of the offender's assets taken, the sanction can range from lenient to fairly stringent—and that proportion could be prescribed in the sentencing standards, commensurately with the seriousness of the offense. The offender would not have to be supervised or forced into proximity with hostile strangers.

The chief difficulty with a system of fines is to operate it even-handedly in a society where wealth is so unequally distributed. But there are possibilities well worth exploring —such as variants of Sweden's "day fine" system, where the offender is fined a percentage of his earnings rather than a flat amount.[5]

Probation[*]—at present the most widely used non-institutional alternative—poses more problems. The idea underlying it is somewhat at odds with our conception: probation means, literally, that the offender is released for a "trial" period to see how well he adjusts: the focus is on improving his future behavior rather than on the character of his past offense.

---

[*] Probation can be unsupervised, when it serves essentially as a suspended sentence—such as was granted to former Vice President Agnew. Or, as is more customary, it is supervised. The probationer is required to abide by specified conditions which require him to report periodically to a probation officer; to refrain from further crimes; to avoid associating with other ex-convicts; and, perhaps, to enroll in a treatment program. Violation of any of the conditions is grounds for revoking his probation and imprisoning him.

Also disturbing are the discretionary features of probation. Probation may be lenient or onerous, depending on the conditions imposed: being required to report to a probation officer once a month is hardly burdensome; being required to enroll in an intensive drug-therapy program is very much more so. Yet this important decision is left wholly to the discretion of the sentencing judge. The offender's probation may be revoked if he violates any of its conditions. Some of the conditions are so vaguely worded that a way can be found to revoke if there is a will. The occasion for revocation may be that the offender is suspected of another crime; or that authorities fear that he might commit another crime in the near future; or that they simply dislike his personal habits or associates. Since revocation means that the offender goes to prison, it is tantamount to a power to imprison at will.*

Yet probation is sometimes used to impose certain restrictions on the offender while he is in the community: he may, for example, be required to limit his travels or observe a curfew. Conceivably, these restrictions could expressly be prescribed as the penalty for certain offenses, detached from the discretionary features and treatment objectives of probation.

* As long as this discretionary power to revoke remains, no system of sentencing standards such as we have proposed is workable—for it would be all too easy for authorities to use that power to evade the rules. If the sentencing rules provide that a particular offense is not serious enough to warrant a prison sentence, the offender (if already on probation at the time he commits the offense) could be confined anyway—simply by charging him with an infringement of his conditions of release and revoking probation.

15

Variations from the Deserved Sentence: What If One Could Predict or Rehabilitate?

IT IS TIME to return to questions raised at the outset: Should an offender's dangerousness be taken into account in setting sentence, assuming it was possible to predict dangerousness better than one can today? Should his need for rehabilitation be considered, were treatment programs developed that worked? Should deterrence be taken into account, were deterrent effects better known? We shall spell out why our theory would ordinarily rule out these considerations, and we shall see whether there might be exceptions.

Predictive Restraint. We have spoken of the problem of false positives in predicting serious crimes. But suppose that, through development of better data and more refined prediction methods, the false-positive rate could be brought down. Should the state then be entitled to confine the offender longer than is commensurate with the seriousness of his past offense, in order to prevent him from committing predicted future crimes?

It should be apparent by now that the fundamental moral objection to predictive restraint is that it is not deserved. This objection stands even were the prediction of future criminality accurate. An offender does not *deserve* to be punished more severely on account of a crime he is predicted to commit, however likely its occurrence. The very concept of deserved punishment, as we have seen, looks to the person's *past* wrongs. His deserts depend on his choice—on his having chosen to act (and having acted) wrongfully: to the extent that his behavior is merely forecast, there is no such action for which he can be held to blame. (Predictive restraint is different from punishment for creating risks—e.g., for driving recklessly: there, the person is being held criminally liable because of the possible consequences of his actual past behavior. With predictive restraint, in contrast, the offender is being penalized not for creating a risk but for *being* a risk. The past deed which led to the offender's conviction has been completed and its consequences realized—and he should be liable in any case for a penalty commensurate with it. Granted, he may remain inclined to commit further crimes, but he is not blameworthy—and hence should not be additionally punished—for having these inclinations, unless and until he decides to act on them.)

Might there be exceptions? While asserting that commensurate deserts should be the prima-facie basis for allocating penalties, we did say that the principle might conceivably be departed from in extraordinary circumstances. It could be argued that, to preserve a system in which sentences are ordinarily based on offenders' deserts, an exception must be made of a small class of especially fearsome cases: namely, defendants who stand convicted of serious assault crimes and who have extensive records of violence. These cases will be so highly visible and evocative of public anxiety that, arguably, the pressures for isolating such persons would be impossible to resist in any event; and unless express authority to invoke predictive restraint is granted here, the entire structure of "deserved" sentences could become distorted upward. (The issue is not whether such offenders are to be incarcerated but for how long. An offender having such a serious criminal record will, under the principle of commensurate deserts, deserve to be incarcerated in any event. The concern, however, is with his remaining violent after having completed his deserved term.) Were predictive restraint authorized for these special situations, however, that authority should be narrowly defined in the sentencing rules. Without explicit and tightly drawn limits, this "exception" could come to be invoked so indiscriminately as to overwhelm the rule.

The converse of predictive restraint remains to be considered—whether prediction may be used to *reduce* an offender's sentence below that which is deserved. Murder, for example, is a crime with a low recidivism rate.[1] Many murderers could be released immediately after conviction with little likelihood of offending again. Yet such premature release is nevertheless objectionable as disproportionately lenient—as depreciating the blameworthiness of the act and the worth of the victim's life.* And, unlike the situation

---

* See Chapter 8. This argument against early release of "non-dangerous"

where the dangerous offender is held beyond his deserved sentence, premature release would seldom be necessary to prevent further victimization of others in the community: even if the offender is predictably "safe" if released early, what greater risk would there be in holding him to his deserved term?

Rehabilitation. What if rehabilitation worked?

Rehabilitation should be distinguished from helping an offender with his own problems, which we have said ought to be offered on a voluntary basis. We assume the offender may not be forced to accept help, for he is a competent adult entitled to decide what his own best interests are. But rehabilitation, as we defined it, is a means of crime control: changing the offender so that he is less likely to offend again. Compulsion would not automatically be ruled out, since the aim is to protect others, rather than, paternalistically, to help the criminal himself.

Our earlier criticism of rehabilitation was directed at the ineffectiveness of existing programs of treatment. But one cannot predict that treatment will *never* work. Conceivably, success could be achieved among certain classes of offenders—e.g., through improved screening. Given this possibility of effective treatment at some future date, to rely on evidence of present ineffectiveness could backfire. We would then be left without any limitations on the rehabilitative disposition, once programs are found that work.

It should be evident, however, that our rationale does supply limits (irrespective of effectiveness) on the extent to which the disposition of an offender may be decided on

---

offenders assumes, we wish to stress, that the penalties are the modest ones we contemplate.

rehabilitative grounds. The limit is provided by the principle of commensurate deserts. Even if rehabilitation works, basing the sentence on the offender's "need for treatment" falls afoul of the commensurateness principle, for much the same reason that basing the sentence on prediction would: the severity of the disposition is being determined, not by the gravity of what he *has* done and thus deserves, but by what he is expected to do in future if he successfully participates in the treatment program. When an offender deserves only X months of confinement, holding him X plus N months—even if the treatment calls for the extra time—is disproportionately severe in relation to the seriousness of the crime. The fact that the treatment is effective does not eliminate that objection: for the same objection of undeserved severity applies, *pari passu*, to predictive restraint although there is no doubt that that measure effectively prevents the offender from committing further crimes against persons outside.*

Might there be exceptions? We have just suggested an

---

* The two kinds of measures—confinement for treatment, and predictive restraint—are, in fact, very similar. In both cases, an offender who is deemed likely to offend again would be confined for a period longer than he deserves, to prevent him from repeating his offense. The only difference is the particular preventive technique. With confinement for treatment, the object is to dispel the offender's criminal propensities through the treatment more quickly than they might remit of themselves were he merely incapacitated—and hence to permit his earlier release. With predictive restraint, one is simply holding the offender to prevent him from acting out his criminal inclinations. If different groups of offenders are considered, however, confinement for treatment will not necessarily involve shorter periods than predictive restraint. There might be one class of offenders who are not amenable to treatment but whose propensities for criminal behavior spontaneously remit in a year or two; and another class whose dangerousness would not spontaneously remit and who are amenable to treatment, but whose treatment requires five years. In that event, those preventively confined could be released earlier.

argument for predictive restraint in certain exceptional situations, where the offender has already been convicted of serious assault crimes and is thought likely to commit acts of violence in future. Parallel logic would apply here. In those narrowly defined circumstances where one can justify holding a violent offender longer, one could also hold a treatable violent offender longer and treat him.° But rehabilitation gives the state no additional warrant for confining beyond that supplied by predictive restraint; ultimately, the issue is the degree of danger the offender poses.

The reverse situation—releasing an offender early on rehabilitative grounds—presents much the same questions as releasing him early on the basis of a prediction that he is not dangerous. Perhaps one could imagine a treatment program that would cure the serious offender of his criminal tendencies in a few weeks. But releasing him as soon as he completes his cure—like releasing him immediately if he is predicted not to offend again—remains objectionable as disproportionately lenient in relation to the gravity of the crime for which he was convicted.

Assuming the duration of a convicted offender's confinement is not changed, what of requiring him to participate in a (assumedly effective) rehabilitation program during his prescribed term? That would depend on the character of the program. For the treatment's unpleasantness—as well as the duration of confinement—affects the severity of the sentence. Were the program relatively innocuous (no more disagreeable, say, than learning a new skill), there would be

° Provided the treatment itself is not unduly cruel or intrusive; see footnote on next page.

less objection: for that does not materially change the severity of the disposition.* But once the program becomes more unpleasant, it increases the severity of the penalty— and the same questions arise as when the duration of confinement is extended for treatment.†

Deterrence. It remains to be considered whether the penalty for a particular category of offense should ever be increased in the interests of deterrence. At the moment, the question is somewhat academic—for there still is little firm evidence on the deterrent effects of varying the severity of penalties. Even were there such evidence, moreover, it would not be easy to imagine cases where one would really want to raise penalties above what is deserved. If it really is so urgent to deter the offense, why is it not serious? Perhaps, for example, one might wish to punish rationing violations severely were there a grave food shortage. But if food were that short, would not the gravity of the offense be greater?

One class of cases comes to mind. A system of punishments based on offenders' deserts requires certain rules to preserve its existence: imprisoned offenders must not escape; offenders subjected to non-incarceration penalties (e.g., intermittent confinement) must not refuse participation. Unless sanctions backing these rules are sufficient to ensure a reasonable degree of compliance, the entire desert-based system would break down.**

* The sanctions invoked against offenders who refused to participate would also have to be modest.

† Commensurate deserts is not, however, the only constraint on the character of the treatment. Compulsory treatments that are cruel, debilitating, or intrusive should be ruled out on ethical grounds, irrespective of their effectiveness and of the seriousness of the offense involved. See, e.g., Michael H. Shapiro, "Legislating the Control of Behavior Control: Autonomy and the Coercive Use of Organic Therapies," 47 *S. Cal. L. Rev.* 237 (1974).

** Here in other words, a distinction should be observed between the system of

IF WE ALLOW any variations from the deserved sentence, what is to restrict them to such special cases? The critical point is that we are speaking of *exceptions*. There is a qualitative difference between making routine use of utilitarian considerations in sentencing decisions and doing what we are doing: making desert the normal basis for the sentence, and permitting variations from the deserved disposition only in narrowly delineated special cases—and only for the purposes of safeguarding the general rule that the sentence should be deserved. For example, when we suggested that predictive restraint might be necessary for a few especially violent defendants, it was to protect the normal (deserved) sentence from upward distortion. This rationale can hold only if the variations are, indeed, exceptional: once utilitarian sentencing is routinely employed, one cannot speak of the "exception" protecting the rule, for it has consumed it.

---

sanctions (whose severity should be based on desert) and the sanctions necessary to maintain that system (which have to deter sufficiently to keep the system operating). Another illustration of this same distinction can be found in pretrial detention. Suppose one takes the position that there should be no pretrial detention, because a person does not deserve to be deprived of his liberty unless found guilty of an offense. To preserve such a rule, however, it may still be necessary to make at least one exception—for absconders who might otherwise simply absent themselves from trial for any misdeed with which they had been charged. (Absconding is itself a crime, for which someone can be tried and punished. But a determined absconder could simply absent himself also from his trial for absconding; at some point, absconders would have to be held *before* trial to ensure their being available to be tried.)

16

Arraying Penalties
on a Scale

How SHOULD penalties be arrayed on a scale, and what should the overall dimensions of the scale be? Our rationale calls for the construction of a scale of modest dimensions. Penalties, like currency, can become inflated; and in this country, inflation has reached runaway proportions. A substantial deflation must be undertaken.

The internal structure of the scale—that is, the ranking of penalties relative to each other—should be governed by the principle of commensurate deserts.* A presumptive sentence should be prescribed for each gradation of seriousness—with limited discretionary authority to raise or lower it for aggravating or mitigating circumstances.† The scale

---

* Chapter 11. (A few limited exceptions to this rule of deserved sentences were discussed in Chapter 15. Such dispositions should be separately regulated in the sentencing standards.)

† Chapter 12.

should thus consist of an array of presumptive sentences, ranked in severity to correspond to the relative gravity of the offenses involved.

The weight given to prior offenses should *expressly* be built into the scale, with separate presumptive penalties set for first infractions and for repeated violations. Penalties for first offenses can then be scaled down substantially, for the reasons explained.°

The scale should be two-dimensional. The dimensions should be: (1) the seriousness of the crime for which the offender currently stands convicted, and (2) the seriousness of his prior record. (The second factor is, in turn, composed of two variables: the number of his prior convictions and the seriousness of each. But a "seriousness of prior record" rating can readily be developed that combines both of these: the best "prior record" rating would be given someone never previously convicted, and the worst would be given someone with a record of more than one serious offense prior to the current conviction.)

There need be only a few gradations of seriousness, if refined discriminations in relative gravity are not practicable. (Conceivably, there could be as few as five categories— minor, lower intermediate, upper intermediate, lower-range serious, and upper-range serious.) An important advantage of a scale having two dimensions is that it has ample power to differentiate penalties, even if the number of gradations of seriousness is kept small. With five degrees of seriousness and four "prior record" gradations, for example, the scale would have room for twenty different penalty levels.†

° Chapter 10.
† With five seriousness gradations and four "prior record" gradations, the

A scale constructed in this fashion has the further advantage of simplicity. It would not be necessary to devise a lengthy sentencing code specifying a distinct presumptive penalty for each offense. The guidelines could simply list the few gradations of seriousness, and state which categories of crimes fall into which gradations. Knowing the offender's crime and his prior record, one could then consult these guidelines to obtain the applicable seriousness rating and seriousness-of-prior-record rating—and, having these, look

penalty scale would look something like this—with the P's representing the presumptive sentences.

HYPOTHETICAL PENALTY SCALE

	1	2	3	4
5	$P_{5,1}$	$P_{5,2}$	$P_{5,3}$	$P_{5,4}$ (most severe)
4	$P_{4,1}$	$P_{4,2}$	$P_{4,3}$	$P_{4,4}$
3	$P_{3,1}$	$P_{3,2}$	$P_{3,3}$	$P_{3,4}$
2	$P_{2,1}$	$P_{2,2}$	$P_{2,3}$	$P_{2,4}$
1	$P_{1,1}$ (least severe)	$P_{1,2}$	$P_{1,3}$	$P_{1,4}$

Seriousness level of most recent offense

Rating for seriousness of prior record
(based on number and seriousness of prior offenses)

The penalty in the lower left-hand corner ($P_{1,1}$) is that prescribed for someone convicted of a minor offense who had no prior record. It would be the least severe penalty on the scale. That in the lower right-hand corner ($P_{1,4}$) is for the person whose current offense is minor but who had a record of serious prior offenses. (This penalty would be somewhat severer, but not very much so, since the offense of which the defendant now stands convicted is still a minor one.) The penalty in the upper right-hand corner ($P_{5,4}$) is that prescribed for someone convicted of a very serious offense who already had a record of major crimes. It would be the severest on the scale. That in the upper left ($P_{5,1}$) would be for someone convicted of a serious crime who had no prior record. Thus the penalties would increase in severity as one goes from left to right and from bottom to top.

up the indicated presumptive sentence on the two-dimensional scale.

The magnitude of the scale is the next concern. Should the scale, for example, run up to a highest penalty of five years' confinement? or fifteen? or fifty?

While regulating the scale's internal composition in detail, the principle of commensurate deserts sets only certain outer bounds on the scale's magnitude. The upper limit, as we have seen,* is: the scale may not be inflated to the point that the severe sanction of incarceration is visited on non-serious offenses. The lower limit is: the scale may not be deflated so much that the *most* serious offenses receive less-than-severe punishments. Within these limits, there remains considerable choice as to the scale's magnitude— where its overall deterrent effect may be taken into account. The difficulty is the absence of data: the deterrent impact of an untried scale of penalties is not known. It will be necessary to choose the scale's magnitude on the basis of surmise—on a best guess of what its deterrent effect is likely to be. Once a scale has been implemented, with its magnitude chosen in somewhat arbitrary fashion, it can then be altered with experience. If the magnitude selected leads to a substantial rise in overall crime rates,† an upward adjustment can be made (within the upper bounds of commensurate deserts). If no such rise results, it would then be appropriate to experiment with further reductions—

* Chapter 11.

† This measure—the impact on the crime rate—will reflect not only the scale's deterrent effect but (to the extent incarceration is utilized) its incapacitative effects as well (see Chapter 13).

In determining the effect of the scale's magnitude on the crime rate, it will be necessary to try to control for other variables that could have influenced the rates (see Chapter 5).

diminishing the scale's magnitude in stages and observing whether any significant loss of deterrent effect occurs. (Such a step-by-step approach to reducing penalty levels should limit the risk of a large, unexpected jump in the crime rate.)

How, then, should one go about selecting a particular magnitude if the initial choice contains so much guesswork? We would suggest taking into account two factors touched upon earlier. One is our principle of "parsimony," that less intervention is preferred unless a strong case for a greater degree of intervention can be made. The other is the hypothesis of diminishing returns:* once penalties reach modest levels of severity, further increases are unlikely to have much added deterrent usefulness.

With these two factors in mind, we recommend adoption of a scale whose highest penalty (save, perhaps, for the offense of murder) is five years[1]—with sparing use made of sentences of imprisonment for more than three years. If the hypothesis of diminishing returns is correct, the elimination of very long sentences could be undertaken without significant diminution of the overall deterrent usefulness of the system.† [2] (Moreover, the sentences, while shorter, would be more certain—and greater certainty could have some additional deterrent benefits. *All* persons convicted of sufficiently serious offenses would face a period of imprison-

* Chapter 7.

† Even if there is a diminishing *deterrent* effect of increasing severity, a larger magnitude will mean longer prison sentences—and hence some added *incapacitative* effect (see Chapter 13). But we are assuming that this added incapacitative effect will not be very large—at least if the use of incarceration is kept within the bounds of commensurate deserts.

It has been recently claimed—by James Q. Wilson and Reuel Shinnar, among others—that dramatic reductions in crime can be achieved through isolating a larger proportion of offenders for longer periods. The evidence to support these claims remains in dispute, however.

ment—rather than the situation with today's discretionary system, where a few such persons receive lengthy sentences but many other serious offenders only get probation.°) Bearing in mind our principle of parsimony and the fact that any initial choice of magnitude is somewhat arbitrary, we think that keeping most prison sentences well below three years is a risk worth taking. If events proved us wrong and such a scale led to a substantial increase in the crime rate, the magnitude of scale could still be adjusted upward, subject to the desert-imposed limit that incarceration could be used only for offenses that were serious.

Sentence Levels. Thus far, we have spoken only of the overall dimensions and formal characteristics of the scale. What kinds of penalties, then, should be imposed for various typical crimes? Answering that would require an assessment of the seriousness of those crimes—thus calling for criteria of seriousness, which we have not supplied. We can, however, offer some surmises, based on our common-sense estimates of seriousness.

Suppose the penalties are those we have suggested: warning-and-release, intermittent confinement, and (for serious offenses only) incarceration. Then sentence levels might run approximately as follows:

1. *Minor offenses* should be punished least severely—by warning-and-release for the first offense, and by a light schedule of intermittent confinement (e.g., a loss of a few Saturdays) for repetitions. Petty thefts would fall in this category.

° For statistics on the relatively low percentage of serious offenders now sent to prison, see, e.g., Adrienne Weir, "The Robbery Offender," in *The Prevention and Control of Robbery*, ed. by Floyd Feeney and Adrienne Weir (Davis, Cal.: U. Cal. at Davis, Center for Administration of Criminal Justice, 1973) (percentage of convicted robbery offenders sent to prison).

2. *Intermediate-level offenses* (from the slightly more than minor to the nearly serious) should be punished mainly by intermittent confinement, although warning-and-release should be used for first offenses in the lower range of this category. For offenses in the upper range, there would be stiff schedules of intermittent confinement involving substantial deprivations of offenders' leisure time. But incarceration should not be employed, since we are still speaking of crimes that do not qualify as serious. Included in this category would be most common thefts of personal belongings which do not involve the threat or risk of violence.

3. *Serious offenses (lower range)* might be punished by intermittent confinement for the first offense, reflecting our conception of a scaled-down penalty for first offenders. Repeated violations, however, should be punished by incarceration. Thefts involving the threat of violence (but not its actual use) would generally fall in this category.

4. *Serious offenses (upper range)* should receive sentences of incarceration in any event. Intentional and unprovoked crimes of violence that cause (or are extremely likely to cause) grave bodily injury to the victim fit here, as would the worst white-collar offenses such as those in which people's lives are knowingly endangered.* [3]

How long should the sentences of confinement be? We

---

* Because of the complexity and variety of the criminal transactions involved, developing seriousness criteria for white-collar offenses will be no easy task. But some white-collar offenses are no less serious than crimes of violence. A striking instance was cited by Willard Gaylin in a recent guest editorial in *The New York Times*: the case of a doctor and drug manufacturer who knowingly sold children's emetics with the active ingredient missing. The emetics were supposed to induce vomiting in children who had accidentally swallowed poison, but would not do so in their adulterated form—so that the child's death could result. The defendant was put on probation. We regard this crime as heinous as shooting at someone with a pistol, and feel it deserves a period of incarceration.

recommend that the presumptive sentences for lower-range serious offenses fall somewhere below eighteen months (with the possible exception of higher sentences—as much as three years, perhaps—for multiple recidivist infractions). Presumptive sentences for upper-range serious offenses would then fall somewhere between eighteen months and three years (except for repeat violations, where sentences could run as high as four and five years). Sentences above five years would be barred altogether—except for certain murders,° and possibly for sentences of predictive restraint in the exceptional circumstances discussed earlier.†

WHEN THIS suggested structure is compared with existing sentencing practice, several major differences emerge.

Under our approach, there will be much less disparity. Defendants having similar criminal records will receive similar dispositions. No longer will it be possible for one offender to be sent to prison for years, while another convicted of a similar crime walks out the courtroom door on probation. Moreover, the defendant will know for

° Murder, the most serious of crimes, presents special problems because of the diverse circumstances under which it is committed. Having a single presumptive penalty might require unduly wide discretionary variations to accommodate killings of varying degrees of gravity. It may be preferable to prescribe separate presumptive penalties for distinct kinds of murder: (1) murders stemming from personal quarrels, (2) unprovoked murders of strangers, (3) political assassinations, and (4) especially heinous murders, such as those involving torture or multiple victims. Five years might be the norm for the personal-quarrel situation, with longer presumptive sentences for the other three categories. This approach would have the additional advantage that the homicides that cause the most public outrage—those in the last three categories—would be dealt with separately: were there only a single presumptive penalty, it would tend to become inflated to accommodate the more shocking homicides.

† See Chapter 15.

certain how much punishment he faces: indeterminacy of sentence is eliminated.

Penalties will be scaled down substantially. Incarceration will be restricted to offenses that are serious—and most prison sentences kept relatively short. (It is true that today the average time served for most major offenses other than murder is less than five years:[4] but those averages conceal many dispositions that are much longer. Our suggested limits on sentences are not averages but true limits.) The reduction in severity would be particularly marked for first offenders.

Severity would thus be substantially reduced, but we emphasize: these suggested punishments would not be so easily avoided. The discretionary features of the existing system allow individuals convicted even of the most serious crimes to be put on suspended sentence or probation. Under our scheme, terms of confinement would be shorter and more sparingly imposed—but a person convicted of a sufficiently serious crime would have to serve the prescribed time.

Lingering Questions

17

Just Deserts in an Unjust Society

WE HAVE scarcely mentioned poverty and social class. In a society in which everyone had ample opportunity to make a decent living within the law, it is comparatively easy to argue that offenders deserve punishment. Difficulty arises when questions of social injustice are taken into account.

To CONSIDER, first, the general justification of punishment: how does social deprivation bear on a desert-based argument for the existence of the criminal sanction? Karl Marx considered this question.* Interestingly enough, he suggests

---

* Marx's writings contain only few (and rather cryptic) comments on the subject of punishment. The view we ascribe here to Marx is based on Jeffrie G. Murphy's interpretation of a passage from Marx's essay "Capital Punishment." Jeffrie G. Murphy, "Marxism and Retribution," 2 *Philosophy & Public Affairs* 217 (1973).

that the *only* morally acceptable ground for punishing is that it is deserved. But a desert-based justification, he argues, is valid only if the laws which punishment upholds are fair—which, in turn, requires an equitably structured society. When the laws of a society reciprocally benefit all its members, the violator may, indeed, be seen as gaining an unjust advantage in profiting from others' compliance while not complying himself. But suppose that the laws serve chiefly the interests of a ruling class at the expense of others.* Where, Marx asks, are the reciprocal benefits which the desert theory assumes? In what sense, then, are violations of the law moral wrongs that deserve to be condemned through punishment?

It is important to note that Marx was *not* arguing for a utilitarian justification of the criminal sanction. Quite the contrary, desert is essential in his view to the case for punishing. His attack is on the underlying social system: as long as that system is unjust, punishment is not defensible.

Whether one accepts or rejects Marx's claims about the inequity of capitalist society, this argument still holds: *If* a society is sufficiently unjust, its institutions of punishment become untenable. Anyone, even an ardent capitalist, could imagine a social system so grossly unfair that he would be hard put to defend punishment under it. Consider, for example, a society in which most persons were literally slaves to a small elite and in which most punishments were

---

* Social injustice can render the laws unjust in a number of different ways. The laws can be written so as to favor the dominant class—e.g., by exempting predatory but profitable behavior from criminal sanctions. Or else, the laws can be administered unfairly: e.g., by not prosecuting affluent offenders. Or else—even if the criminal laws seemed fair on their face and were even-handedly enforced against the affluent and deprived—the latter can be at a disadvantage because their social situation makes it much more difficult to comply.

for acts of disobedience by slaves to their masters: that system of punishment could hardly be defended as deserved—for most punishable acts would in no sense be blameworthy.

Thus, the question comes down to one's view of our society. That social injustice exists in America seems difficult to dispute; but how profoundly does it distort the essentials of the criminal law? Our earlier defense of the existence of punishment necessarily presupposes at least a partial acceptance of this society's laws: one that permits us to consider violators as, by and large, deserving of punishment. A radical social critic might well dispute our assumption and condemn this society and its criminal prohibitions as fundamentally and irretrievably unjust. But the logic of that position leads to opposing the existing institutions of punishment entirely—not to their defense on grounds other than desert.

PROVIDED one accepts the existence of punishment in this society, the next question is that of allocation: *How much* punishment? We have argued that the chief allocation criterion should be the offender's deserts. But how should this criterion deal with questions of social deprivation? Consider the impoverished and alienated ghetto-dweller who turns to crime in the absence of lawful opportunities for making a decent living: what, if any, are his deserts?

The impoverished defendant poses a dilemma for our theory. In principle, a case can be made that he is less culpable—because his deprived status has left him with far fewer opportunities for an adequate livelihood within the law. (H. L. A. Hart points out that, in general, a violator may be deemed less culpable if at the time of the offense he found himself, through no fault of his own, in a situation where "conformity . . . was a matter of special difficulty for him as compared with . . . persons normally placed.")[1] Yet treating "social deprivation" as a mitigating factor raises several formidable practical difficulties:

• What about discretion? Under our scheme, only a limited reduction of sentence is permitted on account of mitigating circumstances. If such limits are observed, the impoverished defendant who is convicted of a very serious crime could still expect severe punishment. On the other hand, if those limits are set aside so as to allow the sentencing judge to cut the penalty substantially, one is reinstituting wide discretion in sentencing, with its attendant evils.

• Is this an issue that judges can be expected to deal with fairly? To decide questions of social deprivation, the judge could not restrict his inquiry to the immediate circumstances of the crime, as he can when he decides conventional issues of mitigation (e.g., whether the defendant was provoked). Instead, he would have to undertake a broad inquiry into the defendant's present situation and past history. And in deciding whether the defendant was sufficiently "deprived" to deserve less punishment, his judgment would tend to be strongly colored by his own social outlook. Perhaps it is asking too much of judges to resolve these questions dispassionately.

• What of the "balloon effect"? If socially deprived offenders are treated as having diminished culpability, will that lead to the expansion of other "non-criminal" modes of control? As the development of the insanity defense suggests,[2] when those who injure others are purportedly exculpated from criminal liability, there tends to be widened use of "civil" commitment having still fewer safeguards.

Given difficulties such as these, it may not be feasible to treat social deprivation as a mitigating factor: the sentencing system may simply not be capable of compensating for the social ills of the wider society.

It is essential, however, that discrimination against the disadvantaged be minimized in the sentencing system. Some discrimination is bound to exist because of the shortcomings of the criminal process prior to conviction: as long as there is unequal access to competent counsel, for example, a poor person is more likely to be convicted of a serious crime than an equally guilty individual of greater means. But one can at least insist that the sentencing system not aggravate the bias that the poor already suffer up to the point of conviction.

Under the commensurate-deserts principle, an impoverished defendant would be punished no more severely than an affluent individual convicted of an equally serious crime—the only uncertainty, as we have seen, is whether he would deserve *less* punishment by reason of his poverty. Utilitarian allocation theories, by contrast, have much greater potential for bias: they could support taking sterner measures against the poor expressly because of their poverty. Were severity of punishment to be based on deterrence, for example, it could be argued that crimes characteristically committed by the poor should be punished more severely: because poor persons, having stronger incentives to commit crimes, require stronger counter-incentives in the form of stern punishments. Theories of predictive restraint have still greater potential for bias. If disposition is to be fashioned to prevent predicted recurrences, it will depend

on the offender's social status. When the public official or
corporation executive commits a serious crime in office, he
can be prevented from doing it again by being removed
from his position of power. The poor person, by contrast,
will lack the opportunity to commit violations such as these.
If he commits a serious offense, it is likely to be with a knife
or pistol, and he will have to go to prison because that
happens to be the only known way of keeping weapons out
of his hands.

But if we wish not to discriminate against the disadvantaged, what of our suggested treatment of prior criminal
record? Once a poor person has committed a crime, does
not the stigma of a prior criminal record compound the
burdens of poverty? And, if so, is not punishing him more
severely if he commits another crime blaming him unfairly
for disabilities which society has helped impose? It is
unquestionably true that the stigma of a criminal record
narrows the person's opportunities. But such disabilities are
the consequences of the person's *own* actions in having
violated the law. From the point of view of the impoverished, moreover, our suggested treatment of prior record
has an important advantage: by scaling down the penalties
for first offenses, we make it easier for him to avoid severe
punishment—he will not suffer the full rigors of the law
unless he strays several times. Were our suggested treatment of prior record rejected and each successive infraction
punished equally, he would be visited by the full penalty
when he made his first mistake.* For an indigent person

---

* The stigma problem would be worse also. Since he will be punished more
severely on the first offense, he will immediately suffer the greater stigma—making
it all the harder to find a lawful livelihood. By scaling down the penalty for the first
offender, we reduce the social disabilities he labors under after his first conviction.

whose restricted opportunities create greater temptations to break the law, one mistake is all too easy to make.

BUT IT should be only small comfort that our theory of punishment deals somewhat less unfairly with deprived persons than traditional utilitarian theories do. As long as a substantial segment of the population is denied adequate opportunities for a livelihood, any scheme for punishing must be morally flawed.

Notes

Chapter 1

1. See David J. Rothman, *The Discovery of the Asylum* (Boston: Little, Brown, 1971), for a history of the development of prisons and other institutions of confinement in the United States.

2. See, e.g., Donald Clemmer, *The Prison Community* (New York: Holt, Rinehart & Winston, 1940); Erving Goffman, *Asylums* (Garden City, N.Y.: Anchor Books, 1961); Gresham M. Sykes, *The Society of Captives* (Princeton: Princeton University Press, 1958).

3. For a historical sketch of judicial intervention in prisons, see David J. Rothman, "Decarcerating Prisoners and Patients," 1 *Civil Liberties Rev.* 8 (1973).

4. Ibid.

5. See, e.g., James O. Robison and Gerald Smith, "The Effectiveness of Correctional Programs," 17 *Crime and Delinquency* 67 (1971); Robert Martinson, "What Works?—Questions and Answers about Prison Reform," *The Public Interest*, Spring 1974, p. 22.

6. See, e.g., Francis A. Allen, *The Borderland of Criminal Justice* (Chicago: University of Chicago Press, 1964); American Friends Service

Committee, *Struggle for Justice* (New York: Hill & Wang, 1971); Rothman, "Decarcerating Prisoners and Patients," *supra* note 3.

7. See, e.g., Norval Morris, *The Future of Imprisonment* (Chicago: University of Chicago Press, 1974). Morris lists, as one of his principles of sentencing, that of "parsimony"—the presumption in favor of the "least restrictive" sanction (pp. 60–61).

Part I

1. Council of Judges, National Council on Crime and Delinquency, *Model Sentencing Act*, Second Edition, reprinted in 18 *Crime and Delinquency* 335 (1972) [hereafter cited as *Model Sentencing Act*], §1.

2. See, e.g., *Model Sentencing Act*; National Advisory Commission on Criminal Justice Standards and Goals, *Corrections* (Washington, D.C.: Government Printing Office, 1973) [hereafter cited as NACCJSG, *Corrections*].

Chapter 2

1. American Law Institute, *Model Penal Code* (Proposed Official Draft, 1962) [hereafter cited as *Model Penal Code*], §7.01(1)(b). For citations in footnote: American Bar Association, Project on Minimum Standards for Criminal Justice, *Sentencing Alternatives and Procedures* (New York: American Bar Association, 1968), §2.5(c); National Commission on Reform of Federal Criminal Laws, *Proposed New Federal Criminal Code* (Washington, D.C.: Government Printing Office, 1971), §3101(2); NACCJSG, *Corrections*, Standard 5.2.

2. For citations in footnote: Allen, *Borderland of Criminal Justice, supra* note 6 to Chapter 1; American Friends Service Committee, *Struggle for Justice, supra* note 6 to Chapter 1; Rothman, "Decarcerating Prisoners and Patients," *supra* note 3 to Chapter 1.

3. For citations in footnote: Zimring's critique of the Manhattan Court Employment Project is set forth in Franklin E. Zimring, "Measuring the Impact of Pretrial Diversion from the Criminal Justice System," 41 *U. Chi. L. Rev.* 224 (1974). For critiques of the California study, see Robison and Smith, "The Effectiveness of Correctional Programs," *supra* note 5 to Chapter 1.

4. Our conclusions about the effectiveness of correctional-treatment programs are based on a summary of effectiveness studies prepared for our Committee by a former senior staff member, David Greenberg. David

F. Greenberg, "Much Ado About Little: The Correctional Effects of Corrections," Department of Sociology, New York University, June 1974 (unpublished) [hereafter referred to as Greenberg, "Much Ado"].

Several published analyses draw similar (predominantly negative) conclusions about the effectiveness of treatment programs. See Robison and Smith, *supra* note 3; Robert Martinson, "What Works?" *supra* note 5 to Chapter 1; and Douglas Lipton, Robert Martinson, and Judith Wilks, *Effectiveness of Correctional Treatment: A Survey of Treatment Evaluation Studies* (New York: Praeger, 1975).

5. Greenberg, "Much Ado," pp. 33–37.

6. Greenberg, "Much Ado," p. 15; Robison and Smith, *supra* note 3, pp. 68–70. Martinson, *supra* note 4, pp. 40–42.

7. Greenberg, "Much Ado," pp. 14, 38–42.

8. Greenberg, "Much Ado," pp. 23–25.

9. R. Dickover, N. E. Maynard, and J. A. Painter, "A Study of Vocational Training in the California Department of Corrections," Cal. Dept. of Corrections, Research Report No. 40, 1971, p. 10.

10. Greenberg, "Much Ado," p. 23.

11. Greenberg, "Much Ado," pp. 25–27.

12. Greenberg, "Much Ado," pp. 12–13 (diversion); pp. 17–22 (probation plus non-residential programs). Martinson, *supra* note 4, pp. 38–40.

13. See, e.g., National Institute of Mental Health, Crime and Delinquency Topics, *Community-Based Correctional Programs* (Rockville, Md.: National Institute of Mental Health, 1971), pp. 33–37.

14. For citations in footnote: see Lloyd W. McCorkle, Albert Elias, and F. Lovell Bixby, *The Highfields Story* (New York: Henry Holt, 1958); Lovick C. Miller, "Southfields: Evaluation of a Short-Term Inpatient Treatment Center for Delinquents," 16 *Crime and Delinquency* 350 (1970); Kentucky Child Welfare Research Foundation, "Community Rehabilitation of the Younger Delinquent Boy: Parkland Non-Residential Group Center," Report to U.S. Dept. of Health, Education and Welfare, 1967.

15. Leslie T. Wilkins, *Evaluation of Penal Measures* (New York: Random House, 1969), pp. 94–98.

16. For study cited in footnote: Gene Kassebaum, David A. Ward, and Daniel M. Wilner, *Prison Treatment and Parole Survival* (New York: John Wiley, 1971).

17. Note, "Conditioning and Other Technologies Used to 'Treat?' 'Rehabilitate?' 'Demolish?' Prisoners and Mental Patients," 45 *S. Cal. L. Rev.* 616 (1973) (use of aversion therapy in California prisons).

18. Ibid.

19. See, e.g., Note, "Aversion Therapy: Its Limited Potential for Use in the Correctional Setting," 26 *Stanford L. Rev.* 1327 (1974).

For citation in footnote: Ralph K. Schwitzgebel, *Development and Legal Regulation of Coercive Behavior Modification Techniques with Offenders* (Chevy Chase, Md.: National Institute of Mental Health, 1971), p. 15.

Chapter 3

The major argument in this chapter—that it is unfair to base criminal sentences on predictions of offenders' likelihood of recidivism, because of the tendency of such forecasts to yield large numbers of false positives— is found in a 1972 article by the principal author: Andrew von Hirsch, "Prediction of Criminal Conduct and Preventive Confinement of Convicted Persons," 21 *Buffalo L. Rev.* 717 (1972). The Committee wishes also to acknowledge its particular indebtedness to one of its members, Alan Dershowitz, who has been exploring the role of predictions of deviant conduct in the law; see, e.g., Alan M. Dershowitz, "The Law of Dangerousness: Some Fictions about Predictions," 23 *J. Legal Ed.* 24 (1970); Alan M. Dershowitz, "The Origins of Preventive Confinement in Anglo-American Law—Part I: The English Experience," 43 *U. Cinc. L. Rev.* 1 (1974).

For a similar argument against basing sentences on predictions of dangerousness, see Morris, *The Future of Imprisonment, supra* note 7 to Chapter 1, ch. 3.

1. *Model Penal Code*, §7.01(1)(a).

For citation in footnote: *Model Penal Code*, §7.03.

2. *Model Sentencing Act*, §§1, 5, 9.

3. For a description of the use of prediction by sentencing judges, see, e.g., Robert O. Dawson, *Sentencing* (Boston: Little, Brown, 1969). Dawson notes that, in granting probation, the "focus is primarily upon the likelihood that the defendant will violate the criminal law if placed on probation, and the question is whether the defendant will be able to lead a law-abiding life if he is given the assistance of probation supervision" (p. 80).

For a discussion of the use of prediction in parole decisions, see, e.g., David T. Stanley, *Prisoners among Us: The Problem of Parole*, The Brookings Institution, Washington, D.C., April 1975 (pre-publication draft); Citizens' Inquiry on Parole and Criminal Justice, *Prison without Walls: A Report on New York Parole* (New York: Praeger, 1975).

4. Illustrative of the link between the ideas of rehabilitation and predictive restraint is the statement by Zebulon R. Brockway, "The Ideal of a True Prison System for a State," National Congress on Penitentiary and Reformatory Discipline, *Transactions* (1870), p. 54. "No man, be he judge, lawyer or layman, can determine beforehand the date when imprisonment shall work reformation in any case, and it is an outrage upon society to return to the privileges of citizenship those who have proved themselves dangerous and bad by the commission of crime, until a cure is wrought and reformation reached. . . . Therefore . . . sentences should not be determinate, but *indeterminate*. By this is meant (to state briefly) *that all persons in a state, who are convicted of crimes or offences before a competent court, shall be deemed wards of the state, and shall be committed to the custody of the board of guardians, until, in their judgment, they may be returned to society with ordinary safety, and in accord with their own highest welfare.*" (Emphasis in original.)

5. Support for predictive restraint alone, without rehabilitation, is found in the 1973 report of the National Advisory Commission on Criminal Justice Standards and Goals, NACCJSG, *Corrections*, Commentary on Standard 5.3: ". . . there are some offenders whose aggressive, repetitive, violent, or predatory behavior poses a serious threat to the community. In many instances, these offenders are not responsive to correctional programs. Public safety may require that they be incapacitated for a period of time in excess of 5 years."

A 1974 statement by William Saxbe, then the United States Attorney General, also exemplifies this philosophy. In a reported speech to the International Association of Chiefs of Police, he said: " 'Too many dangerous convicted offenders are placed back in society in one way or another, and that simply must stop.' . . . Mr. Saxbe departed from his prepared text to deliver a free-wheeling attack on 'starry-eyed' theorists whose view of prison as an instrument of rehabilitation . . . results in the return to society of dangerous, hardened criminals with no intention of going straight. . . . 'Prosecutors, court and parole boards must face the fact that some violent offenders cannot be rehabilitated,' he declared. 'Dangerous and violent offenders . . . should know that arrest means conviction and conviction means prison.' " "Saxbe and Kelley, Citing Crime Rise, Hold Prosecutors and Courts Guilty," *New York Times*, Sept. 24, 1974, p. 18.

6. *Model Sentencing Act*, preface.

7. Alan M. Dershowitz, "The Law of Dangerousness: Some Fictions about Predictions," 23 *J. Legal Ed.* 24, 26 (1970).

8. E. W. Burgess, "Factors Determining Success or Failure on Parole," in *The Workings of The Indeterminate Sentence Law of Illinois,* ed. by A. A. Bruce, A. G. Haino, and E. W. Burgess (Springfield, Ill.: State Board of Parole, 1928).

9. Wilkins, *Evaluation of Penal Measures, supra* note 15 to Chapter 2, ch. 5.

10. For citation in footnote: Albert Rosen, "Detection of Suicidal Patients: An Example of Some Limitations in the Prediction of Infrequent Events," 18 *J. Consulting Psychol.* 397 (1954).

See also Alan M. Dershowitz, "Preventive Disbarment: The Numbers Are against It," 58 *Amer. Bar Ass'n J.* 815 (1972). In his article, Dershowitz analyzed a preventive disbarment scheme proposed by a committee of the American Bar Association. That committee had suggested the establishment of a prediction test for law-school applicants, designed to screen out those likely to engage in professional misconduct were they to become lawyers. From available statistics, Dershowitz estimated that those lawyers eventually disciplined would constitute no more than five percent of the first-year students entering law school in any given year. With violations so infrequent, a predictive index would forecast many more false positives than true. If, for example, the test successfully forecasted about half the actual violators, it would incorrectly identify *four times* as many non-violators as candidates for preventive disbarment. He concluded: "As long as we are dealing with a population that includes so small a proportion of future violators, it will not be possible to spot any significant proportion of those violators without erroneously including a far larger number of 'false positives.' This, in a nutshell, is the dilemma of attempting to predict rare human occurrences" (p. 819).

11. Ernst A. Wenk and James O. Robison, "Assaultive Experience and Assaultive Potential," National Council on Crime and Delinquency Research Center, Davis, Cal., 1971 (unpublished monograph); findings subsequently published in Ernst A. Wenk and Robert L. Emrich, "Assaultive Youth: An Exploratory Study of the Assaultive Experience and Assaultive Potential of California Youth Authority Wards," 9 *J. Research in Crime and Delinquency* 171 (1972).

12. For citation in footnote: Harry L. Kozol, Richard J. Boucher, and Ralph F. Garofalo, "The Diagnosis and Treament of Dangerousness," 18 *Crime and Delinquency* 371 (1972).

13. The false-positive rate will decline as the "base rate" (that is, the rate in the sample of the events to be predicted) approaches 50 percent.

See Paul E. Meehl and Albert Rosen, "Antecedent Probability and the Efficiency of Psychometric Signs, Patterns and Cutting Scores," 52 *Psychol. Bull.* 194 (1955).

14. Wenk-Robison-Emrich, *supra* note 11.

15. For citations in footnote: The Winship decision: *In re Winship*, 397 U.S. 358 (1970); rulings on jury unanimity: *Johnson* v. *Louisiana*, 406 U.S. 356 (1972); *Apodaca* v. *Oregon*, 406 U.S. 404 (1972).

Chapter 4

For a useful general critique of "individualized" sentencing, see Marvin E. Frankel, *Criminal Sentences* (New York: Hill & Wang, 1972).

See also Willard Gaylin, *Partial Justice* (New York: Alfred A. Knopf, 1974). Gaylin examines judges' varying philosophies of punishment and suggests how these different philosophies result in divergent outcomes in similar cases.

For the problems of structuring discretion generally, see Kenneth Culp Davis, *Discretionary Justice* (Urbana, Ill.: University of Illinois Press, 1971).

1. See, e.g., Z. R. Brockway, "The Ideal of a True Prison System for a State," *supra* note 4 to Chapter 3.

2. Support for "individualized" sentencing for community treatment is found, for example, in the report of the National Advisory Commission on Criminal Justice Standards and Goals. NACCJSG, *Corrections*, ch. 5.

3. Conn. Gen. Stats. Ann. §§53a–34, 53a–35, 53a–134.

4. See, e.g., Marvin E. Frankel, *Criminal Sentences* (New York: Hill & Wang, 1972), ch. 4.

5. See, e.g., Stanley, *Prisoners among Us, supra* note 3 to Chapter 3; Citizens' Inquiry, *Prison without Walls, supra* note 3 to Chapter 3.

For citations in footnote: The rules of the U.S. Board of Parole are set forth in United States Board of Parole, "Parole, Release, Supervision and Recommitment of Prisoners, Youth Offenders, and Juvenile Delinquents," 28 C.F.R. §§2.1–2.57 (1974). See also Robert Wool, "The New Parole and the Case of Mr. Simms," *New York Times Magazine*, July 29, 1973, p. 14. For a more critical analysis of the Board's rules, see Project, "Parole Release Decision-making and the Sentencing Process," 84 *Yale L. J.* 810 (1975).

The new guidelines of the California parole board were published in a March 1, 1975, memorandum to all California inmates by the chairman of the board, R. D. Procunier. State of California, Adult Authority, "Parole

Consideration Hearing Procedures," Sacramento, Cal., March 1, 1975 (unpublished memorandum).

6. There have been numerous studies of disparity in sentencing; a useful recent summary and analysis of many of these is set forth in John Hagan, "Extra-Legal Attributes and Criminal Sentencing: An Assessment of a Sociological Viewpoint," 8 *Law & Society Review* 357 (1974).

7. Anthony Partridge and William B. Eldridge, *The Second Circuit Sentencing Study: A Report to the Judges of the Second Circuit* (Washington, D.C.: Federal Judicial Center, August 1974).

8. Willard Gaylin, *Partial Justice* (New York: Alfred A. Knopf, 1974), pp. 162, 165.

9. Caleb Foote, "The Sentencing Function," in *A Program for Prison Reform* (Cambridge, Mass.: Roscoe Pound-American Trial Lawyers Foundation, 1972), p. 32.

10. Ibid.

11. See New York Special Commission on Attica, *Attica* (New York: Bantam Books, 1972). The commission found that one of the major factors contributing to inmates' discontent at the time of the 1971 Attica uprising was the uncertainty concerning release dates which resulted from sentence indeterminacy. See also Frankel, *supra* note 4, p. 89. "We have subjected the supposed beneficiaries of the rehabilitative process to a hated regime of uncertainty and helplessness, ignoring that a program of 'cures' thus imposed is doomed from its inception."

12. See, e.g., Frankel, *supra* note 4, ch. 7.

13. Ibid.

14. See, e.g., Note, "Appellate Review of Primary Sentencing Decisions: A Connecticut Case Study," 69 *Yale L. J.* 1451 (1961).

15. Frankel, *supra* note 4, pp. 70–71.

16. For citation in footnote: Note, "Appellate Review of Primary Sentencing Decisions," *supra* note 14, p. 1477.

17. For citation in footnote: *Model Penal Code* (Tentative Draft No. 2, 1954), comment to §1.02, p. 4.

Part II

1. For a discussion of the definition of punishment, see, e.g., H. L. A. Hart, "Prolegomenon to the Principles of Punishment," in his *Punishment and Responsibility* (New York: Oxford University Press, 1968), ch. 1. But see Tziporah Kasachkoff, "The Criteria of Punishment: Some Neglected Considerations," 2 *Canadian J. Philosophy* 363 (1973).

2. H. L. A. Hart, "Prolegomenon," *supra* note 1.

Chapter 5

For a general introduction to the concept of deterrence, see Franklin E. Zimring and Gordon J. Hawkins, *Deterrence* (Chicago: University of Chicago Press, 1973). Also Johannes Andenaes, *Punishment and Deterrence* (Ann Arbor: University of Michigan Press, 1974).

1. See, e.g., Jeremy Bentham, "An Introduction to the Principles of Morals and Legislation," in *The Works of Jeremy Bentham*, ed. by John Bowring (New York: Russell & Russell, 1962), vol. 1.

2. See Leon Radzinowicz, *Ideology and Crime* (New York: Columbia University Press, 1966), pp. 50–56.

As recently as 1959, the assertion could be found in a standard criminology text that "the claim for deterrence is belied by both history and logic." Harry E. Barnes and Negley K. Teeters, *New Horizons in Criminology*, 3rd ed. (Englewood Cliffs, N.J.: Prentice-Hall, 1959), p. 286.

3. See, e.g., Johannes Andenaes, "The General Preventive Effects of Punishment," 114 *U. Pa. L. Rev.* 949 (1966).

4. Oliver Wendell Holmes, *The Common Law*, ed. by Mark DeWolfe Howe (Boston: Little, Brown, 1963), p. 40.

5. For citation in footnote: Franklin E. Zimring and Gordon J. Hawkins, *Deterrence* (Chicago: University of Chicago Press, 1973), p. 74.

6. For citation in footnote: Andenaes, "The General Preventive Effects of Punishment," *supra* note 3, pp. 950–51, 959–60.

7. Studies which support the conclusion that the death penalty does not measurably reduce homicide rates by comparison with long prison sentences include Karl Schuessler, "The Deterrent Effect of the Death Penalty," 284 *Annals* 54 (1952); and Thorsten Sellin, *Capital Punishment* (New York: Harper & Row, 1967). However, the economist Isaac Ehrlich, in a recent, much-disputed study, has argued that the death penalty does have substantial deterrent effect (Isaac Ehrlich, "The Deterrent Effect of Capital Punishment: A Question of Life and Death," 65 *American Economic Review* 397 [1975]).

8. For citations in footnote: Gordon Tullock, "Does Punishment Deter Crime?" *The Public Interest*, Summer 1974, pp. 103, 104. For some more skeptical comments, see David F. Greenberg, "Theft, Rationality and Deterrence Research," Department of Sociology, New York University, July 1974 (unpublished, prepared for presentation at the 1975 Annual Meeting of the American Sociological Association).

9. H. Laurence Ross, "Law, Science and Accidents: The British Road Safety Act of 1967," 2 *J. Legal Studies* 1 (1973).

10. H. Laurence Ross, "The Scandinavian Myth: The Effectiveness of
Drinking-and-Driving Legislation in Sweden and Norway," 4 *J. Legal
Studies* __ (1975) pp. 19–20 (draft version). For citation in footnote:
Ibid., p. 20 (draft version).

11. Zimring and Hawkins, *Deterrence, supra* note 5, pp. 167–69.

12. Johannes Andenaes, "The Morality of Deterrence," 37 *U. Chi. L.
Rev.* 649, 664 (1970).

Chapter 6

While the literature of penology during this century has paid little heed
to the concept of desert, the idea of deserved punishment has received
some attention in philosophical literature. See, e.g., C. W. K. Mundle,
"Punishment and Desert," 4 *Philosophical Quarterly* 216 (1954); K. G.
Armstrong, "The Retributivist Hits Back," 70 *Mind* 471 (1961); H. J.
McCloskey, "A Non-Utilitarian Approach to Punishment," 8 *Inquiry* 249
(1965); Herbert Morris, "Persons and Punishment," 52 *The Monist* 475
(1968); J. Kleinig, *Punishment & Desert* (The Hague: Nijhoff, 1973).

1. *Oxford English Dictionary*, 1933, vol. 8, p. 581.

2. For citation in footnote: *Model Sentencing Act*, introduction.

3. For discussion of the retrospective focus of deserved punishment,
see, e.g., John Kleinig, "The Concept of Desert," 8 *Am. Philosophical
Quar.* 71 (1971); Joel Feinberg, "Justice and Personal Desert," in his
Doing and Deserving (Princeton: Princeton University Press, 1970), ch. 4.

4. This argument is a synthesis of various (often obscure) passages in
Kant, which has been suggested by Jeffrie G. Murphy in his writings on
Kant. Jeffrie G. Murphy, *Kant: The Philosophy of Right* (London:
Macmillan, 1970), pp. 109–12, 140–44; Jeffrie G. Murphy, "Marxism and
Retribution," 2 *Philosophy & Public Affairs* 218, 228 (1973).

There are, however, other claims Kant makes about punishment which
we do *not* espouse, to wit:

a. Kant asserts that desert is both necessary and sufficient to justify the
existence of punishment. Ibid. We argue that it is a necessary but not a
sufficient ground for the criminal sanction—for the reasons we set forth
later in this chapter.

b. As to *how much* punishment the offender deserves, Kant subscribes
to the *lex talionis*: the offender should suffer as much injury as he inflicted
on the victim, and, where possible, the injury should be of the same kind
(Immanuel Kant, *Rechtslehre*, Hastie translation, excerpted in *Philosophical Perspectives on Punishment*, ed. by Gertrude Ezorsky [Albany: State

University of New York Press, 1972], pp. 103–6). As the reader will see in Chapters 8 and 11, we do not espouse the *lex talionis*: the severity of the punishment, we hold, should be proportional to the gravity of the offense, but the proportion may be less than "an eye for an eye": the penalty need not inflict as much suffering as the wrong inflicted.

There is nothing inconsistent, it should be noted, in accepting the Kantian argument we rely upon in the text, while rejecting the *lex talionis*. The argument we rely upon is that punishment cancels the unfair advantage which the offender has obtained over all his fellow citizens when he fails to respect others' rights while benefiting from their non-interference with his rights. The advantage, then, is not that gained by the offender over his victim; but over *any* law-abiding citizen (victimized or not) who has limited his own conduct so as not to interfere with others' rights. Since the focus is on the offender's position vis-à-vis *all* other citizens, rather than on the victim alone, the quantum of punishment would not necessarily have to equal the victim's suffering.

5. Herbert Morris, "Persons and Punishment," 52 *The Monist* 475, 478 (1968).

6. For citations in footnote: Joel Feinberg, "The Expressive Function of Punishment," in his *Doing and Deserving, supra* note 3, ch. 5; Henry M. Hart, Jr., "The Aims of the Criminal Law," 23 *Law & Contemp. Prob.* 401 (1958).

For further comments on reprobation as a justification for punishment, see H. L. A. Hart, "Postscript: Responsibility and Retribution," in his *Punishment and Responsibility* (New York: Oxford University Press, 1968), ch. 9.

7. For citation in footnote: Feinberg, "The Expressive Function of Punishment," *supra* note 6.

7a. Ibid., pp. 102–4.

8. See, e.g., John Rawls, *A Theory of Justice* (Cambridge, Mass.: Belknap Press of Harvard University Press, 1971), pp. 22–27.

9. For citations in footnote: Robert Nozick, *Anarchy, State and Utopia* (New York: Basic Books, 1974); Peter Singer, "The Right to be Rich or Poor," *New York Review of Books*, March 6, 1975, p. 19.

10. Rawls, *supra* note 8, pp. 3–4.

11. For citation in footnote: H. L. A. Hart, "Prolegomenon to the Principles of Punishment" in his *Punishment and Responsibility, supra* note 6, ch. 1.

12. Holmes, *The Common Law, supra* note 4 to Chapter 5, p. 36.

Part III

Chapter 7

1. Cesare Beccaria, *Of Crimes and Punishments*, trans. by Henry Paolucci (New York: Bobbs-Merrill, 1963), p. 58.

2. A number of these studies are summarized in George Antunes and A. Lee Hunt, "The Deterrent Impact of Criminal Sanctions: Some Implications for Criminal Justice Policy," 51 *J. Urban Law* 145 (1973); and Charles R. Tittle, "Punishment and Deterrence of Deviance," in *The Economics of Crime and Punishment*, ed. by Simon Rottenberg (Washington, D.C.: American Enterprise Institute, 1973), p. 85.

3. Sellin, *Capital Punishment, supra* note 7 to Chapter 5. But for a contrary conclusion, see Ehrlich, *supra* note 7 to Chapter 5.

4. F. K. Beutel, *Some Potentialities of Experimental Jurisprudence as a New Branch of Social Science* (Lincoln: University of Nebraska Press, 1957).

5. Gary S. Becker, "Crime and Punishment: An Economic Approach," 76 *J. Political Economy* 169 (1968). Isaac Ehrlich, "Participation in Illegitimate Activities: An Economic Analysis," 81 *J. Political Economy* 521 (1973). R. A. Carr-Hill and N. H. Stern, "An Econometric Model of the Supply and Control of Recorded Offenses in England and Wales," *J. Public Economics*, November 1973.

6. Ehrlich, "Participation in Illegitimate Activities," *supra* note 5.

7. Ibid.; Carr-Hill and Stern, *supra* note 5.

8. See, e.g., Zimring and Hawkins, *Deterrence, supra* note 5 to Chapter 5; Llad Phillips, "Crime Control: The Case for Deterrence," in *The Economics of Crime and Punishment, supra* note 2, p. 65; Tittle, *supra* note 2, pp. 85, 101.

For citation in footnote: Isaac Ehrlich, "The Deterrent Effect of Criminal Law Enforcement," 1 *J. Legal Studies* 259, 266 (1972).

9. For citation in footnote: Tittle, *supra* note 2, p. 100.

10. See, e.g., Becker, *supra* note 5, and George J. Stigler, "The Optimum Enforcement of Laws," 78 *J. Political Economy* 526 (1970).

For citation in footnote: American Friends Service Committee, *Struggle for Justice, supra* note 6 to Chapter 1, pp. 62–64.

Chapter 8

As explained in this chapter, the principle of commensurate deserts—that the severity of punishment should, as a matter of justice, be commensurate with the seriousness of the offense—has not received much attention in traditional penological literature. There has, however, been some recent interest.

Norval Morris, dean of the University of Chicago Law School, discusses it in his recent book on the aims of sentencing (Norval Morris, *The Future of Imprisonment* [Chicago: University of Chicago Press, 1974], ch. 3). Morris argues that the principle is a requirement of justice that limits the pursuit of utilitarian sentencing aims; he holds that it sets an upper limit (and perhaps, although this is less clear in his book, also a lower limit) on the severity of the punishment for any given offense category. Within these desert-based limits, variations in severity would be allowed for deterrent and certain other utilitarian purposes. Our view of the principle differs somewhat from Morris's, however, as discussed on p. 73 of the text.

M. Kay Harris, associate director of the American Bar Association's Resource Center on Correctional Law and Legal Services, has argued that sentences should be based primarily on the seriousness of the offense, rather than on deterrent, incapacitative, or rehabilitative grounds. M. Kay Harris, "Disquisition on the Need for a New Model for Criminal Sanctioning Systems," 77 *W. Va. L. Rev.* 263 (1975).

With respect to juvenile delinquents, Professor Sanford Fox has urged that sentences be based on desert rather than on traditional rehabilitative notions. Sanford Fox, "The Reform of Juvenile Justice: The Child's Right to Punishment," 25 *Juvenile Justice* 2 (1974).

California's parole board, it also should be noted, has adopted new standards for parole release which rely more heavily than does current law upon the seriousness of the offense in determining the duration of prison terms (State of California, Adult Authority, "Parole Consideration Hearing Procedures," *supra* note 5 to Chapter 4). See also, the governor of Illinois's proposed system of legislatively fixed "flat" sentences (News Release from the Office of the Governor of Illinois, Springfield, Ill., Feb. 18, 1975), which is now pending in the State Legislature.

1. Beccaria, *Of Crimes and Punishments, supra* note 1 to Chapter 7; Radzinowicz, *Ideology and Crime, supra* note 2 to Chapter 5, ch. 1.

2. Ibid. Also Bentham, "An Introduction to the Principles of Morals and Legislation," *supra* note 1 to Chapter 5, pp. 83–84, 86–89.

3. H. Donnedieu de Vabres, *Traité de Droit Criminel et de Législation Comparée* (3rd ed., 1947), pp. 27–28, cited in Radzinowicz, *supra* note 1, p. 24.

4. *Strafgesezbuch für das Koenigreich Baiern* (1813), cited in Radzinowicz, *supra* note 1, p. 23.

5. New Hampshire Constitution of 1784, Bill of Rights, §18.

6. Radzinowicz, *supra* note 1, ch. 2.

7. *Model Sentencing Act*, Introduction and §§1, 5, 9. Also the Act's first edition: Council of Judges, National Council on Crime and Delinquency, *Model Sentencing Act*, reprinted in 9 *Crime and Delinquency* 337 (1963), §§1, 5, 9.

8. For citation in footnote: *In re Lynch*, 8 Cal. 3d. 410, 503 P.2d 921 (Cal. Sup. Ct., 1972.)

9. *Model Penal Code*, §7.01(1)(c).

10. H. L. A. Hart, "Prolegomenon," *supra* note 11 to Chapter 6.

11. See introductory comments to the notes for this chapter.

12. For citation in footnote: Bentham, *supra* note 2, p. 88.

13. For citation in footnote: H. L. A. Hart, "Prolegomenon," *supra* note 10, p. 25.

14. Henry M. Hart, "The Aims of the Criminal Law," *supra* note 6 to Chapter 6.

15. For citation in footnote: Andrew von Hirsch, "Prediction of Criminal Conduct and Preventive Confinement of Convicted Persons," 21 *Buffalo L. Rev.* 717, 746 (1972).

16. See, e.g., K. G. Armstrong, "The Retributivist Hits Back," 70 *Mind* 471 (1961); Zimring and Hawkins, *Deterrence, supra* note 5 to Chapter 5, pp. 40–41.

17. Cf. *Model Penal Code*, §7.01(1)(c), requiring the sanction of imprisonment if a lesser sentence "will depreciate the seriousness of the defendant's crime."

For discussion in footnote: Joel Feinberg makes the same point in his "The Expressive Function of Punishment," *supra* note 6 to Chapter 6, p. 118; see also C. W. K. Mundle, "Punishment and Desert," 4 *Philosophical Quarterly* 216 (1954). The Kantian argument on which we rely in Chapter 6 also does not require "eye for an eye" punishments, for reasons explained in note 4 to Chapter 6.

18. Morris is somewhat unclear as to whether the principle sets lower as well as upper limits on punishment. At one point, he states that "the concept of desert . . . is thus limited in its use as defining the *maximum* of punishment that the community exacts from the criminal to express the severity of the injury his crime inflicted on the community" Morris, *The Future of Imprisonment, supra* note 7 to Chapter 1, p. 74 (emphasis added). But elsewhere in his book, he adopts the Model Penal Code's principle that the severity of the punishment may not fall so low as to "depreciate the seriousness of the crime(s) committed"—which seems to set a *lower* limit on severity, based on the idea of desert (Ibid., p. 60).

19. *Model Sentencing Act*, introduction.

20. See, e.g., *Model Penal Code* §7.01; Frankel, *Criminal Sentences, supra* note 4 to Chapter 4, pp. 108–11.

Chapter 9

1. Thorsten Sellin and Marvin E. Wolfgang, *The Measurement of Delinquency* (New York: John Wiley & Sons, 1964).

2. G. N. G. Rose, "Concerning the Measurement of Delinquency," 6 *British J. Criminology* 414 (1966).

3. Peter H. Rossi *et al.*, "The Seriousness of Crimes: Normative Structure and Individual Differences," 39 *Am. Sociological Rev.* 224 (1974).

4. Ibid., pp. 231, 237.

Chapter 10

1. Is punishing the repeat offender more severely than the first offender a matter of deserts? Traditionally, the question did not seem important, because the whole idea of commensurate deserts was not taken seriously. Even among recent writers who give more prominence to the commensurate-deserts principle, however, this issue has received little attention. While Norval Morris argues that a person who returns to crime after having previously been punished should be penalized more severely, he views this as a principle which is separate from notions of desert and is based on utilitarian objectives of crime control (Morris, *The Future of Imprisonment, supra* note 7 to Chapter 1, pp. 60, 79–80). M. Kay Harris, arguing that sentences should be based on offenders' deserts, states flatly—but without elaborating reasons—that prior convictions should *not* be taken into account at all in setting sentence (M. Kay Harris, "Disquisition on the Need for a New Model for Criminal Sanctioning Systems," 77 *W. Va. L. Rev.* 263, 324 [1975]).

2. See, e.g., Daniel Katkin, "Habitual Offender Laws: A Reconsideration," 21 *Buffalo L. Rev.* 99 (1971). Also, New York State's "second felony offender" law, which went into effect January 1, 1973, provides that any offender who has committed a second felony (the first having been committed in any jurisdiction) will automatically be imprisoned, with long mandatory minima prescribed (N.Y. Penal Law §70.06).

For citation in footnote: for example, in the District of Columbia, a third offense of theft of over $100 can result in a sentence of life imprisonment. See D.C. Code §§22–2201, 22–104a.

3. United States Board of Parole, "Parole, Release, Supervision and Recommitment of Prisoners, Youth Offenders, and Juvenile Delinquents," *supra* note 5 to Chapter 4.

4. See, e.g., Don M. Gottfredson, "The Base Expectancy Approach," in *The Sociology of Punishment & Correction*, ed. by Norman Johnston, Leonard Savitz, and Marvin E. Wolfgang (New York: John Wiley, 1970), p. 807.

Part IV

Chapter 12

Methods of structuring and limiting sentencing discretion have attracted much recent interest; and (as noted in the introductory paragraphs to the notes to Chapter 8) some jurisdictions have recently adopted or proposed standards for sentencing or parole that reduce sentencing judges' and parole boards' dispositional leeway.

The manner in which discretion is limited will depend, in important part, on the choice of sentencing objectives. In his book, *Criminal Sentences*, Marvin Frankel assumes at least four goals—desert, deterrence, predictive restraint, and rehabilitation—and thus opts for a "two-track" sentencing system in which some sentences would be determinate (namely, those designed to visit offenders with their deserts or achieve deterrence) and some would be indeterminate (namely, those intended to rehabilitate or restrain the dangerous) (Frankel, *Criminal Sentences*, *supra* note 4 to Chapter 4, pp. 105–11). The limits on sentencing discretion we suggest in this chapter are based on our rather different conception: that only desert ought ordinarily to determine the choice of sentence. As we exclude considerations of predictive restraint and rehabilitation, we can have narrower limits on sentencing discretion than Judge Frankel would; and we have no need at all for indeterminacy of sentence.

1. Frankel, *Criminal Sentences*, *supra* note 4 to Chapter 4, p. 109.

For citation in footnote: Morris, *The Future of Imprisonment*, *supra* note 7 to Chapter 1, p. 48.

2. The New York legislature enacted in 1973 a sweeping revision of the state's penalty structure, which mandated terms of imprisonment for many major felonies. Minimum required prison terms range from one year to as much as fifteen years, depending on the offense. N.Y. Penal Law §§55.00–70.40.

3. See, e.g., American Bar Association Project on Standards for Criminal Justice, *Appellate Review of Sentences* (Approved Draft) (New York: American Bar Association, 1968); Frankel, *Criminal Sentences, supra* note 1, pp. 75–85.

4. For citation in footnote: Don M. Gottfredson, Leslie T. Wilkins, and Jack M. Kress, Project on Sentencing in State Courts, Criminal Justice Research Center, Inc., Albany, N.Y.

5. See note 5 to Chapter 4.

6. Judge Frankel has proposed the creation of a special administrative rule-making body which would be responsible for setting sentencing standards (subject, however, to a legislative veto) (Frankel, *Criminal Sentences, supra* note 1, pp. 118–23). Ours is a variant of his idea—to create a special rule-making agency under the aegis of the *courts* to set the standards.

7. For a description of some of the common abuses of plea-bargaining, see, e.g., Albert W. Alschuler, "The Prosecutor's Role in Plea Bargaining," 36 *U. Chi. L. Rev.* 50 (1968).

8. See, e.g., American Friends Service Committee, *Struggle for Justice, supra* note 6 to Chapter 1; National Advisory Commission on Criminal Justice Standards and Goals, *Courts* (Washington, D.C.: Government Printing Office, 1973), p. 46.

9. See, e.g., Note, "Restructuring the Plea Bargain," 82 *Yale L. J.* 286 (1972). But see Joseph Goldstein, "For Harold Lasswell: Some Reflections on Human Dignity, Entrapment, Informed Consent, and the Plea Bargain," 84 *Yale L. J.* 683 (1975).

10. See notes 8 and 9.

Chapter 13

1. Goffman, *Asylums, supra* note 2 to Chapter 1, pp. 5–6.

2. For citations in footnote: Board of Directors, National Council on Crime and Delinquency, "The Nondangerous Offender Should Not Be Imprisoned," 19 *Crime and Delinquency* 449, 455 (1973); *Model Penal Code*, §301.1(2)(e).

3. Goffman, *Asylums, supra* note 1, pp. 67–68.

4. Terence Morris and Pauline Morris, *Pentonville: A Sociological Study of an English Prison* (London: Routledge & Kegan Paul, 1963), p. 168.

5. For citations in footnote: The cited study showing no criminogenic effect is John E. Berecochea, Dorothy R. Jaman, and Welton A. Jones,

"Time Served in Prison and Parole Outcome: An Experimental Study," Research Report No. 49, Research Div., Cal. Dept. of Corrections, October 1973. The study took a population of imprisoned offenders in California (those who received a parole date during March–August 1970) and, at random, assigned them to an experimental and a control group. The controls served six months longer than the experimentals. No difference in the recidivism rate of the two groups was found. The authors interpreted these findings optimistically: time served in prison may be reduced without affecting the inmates' subsequent level of recidivism. But the reverse is equally true: that prisoners held *longer* did not recidivate more often, the prisons-are-schools-for-crime notion notwithstanding. The effects of longer variations in time served, however, are not tested in this study.

6. David J. Rothman, "Doing Time: Days, Months and Years in the Criminal Justice System," Pinkerton Lecture delivered at the School of Criminal Justice, State University of New York at Albany, March 6, 1974 (unpublished).

7. Goffman, *Asylums, supra* note 1, pp. 67–69.

8. For materials in footnote: The Supreme Court has not yet decided whether the imposition of bail in excess of a defendant's ability to pay constitutes excessive bail. Most jurisdictions take the view that it does not. See, e.g., Temporary Commission on the New York State Court System, . . . *And Justice for All: Part II* (New York: Temporary Commission on the State Court System, January 1973), ch. 6.

9. American Friends Service Committee, *Struggle for Justice, supra* note 6 to Chapter 1, pp. 98–99.

Chapter 14

1. Proposed alternatives to incarceration, in recent years, have often taken the form of diversion (where criminal charges against an accused are dropped on condition that he agree to participate in a treatment program) or community-based treatment and supervision programs. The National Advisory Commission on Criminal Justice Standards and Goals, for example, states that diversion "gives society the opportunity to consider the possibility of reallocating existing resources to programs that promise greater success in bringing about correctional reform and social restoration of offenders," and proposes "development of a systematic plan for creation of varied community-based programs that will best respond to the range of offender needs and community interests."

NACCJSG, *Corrections*, pp. 77, 237; and generally, Ibid., Standards 3.1 and 7.1.

2. See, e.g., N.Y. Penal Law §65.20.

3. Materials in footnote: For description of use of intermittent confinement in Western Europe, see Great Britain, Home Office, *Custodial and Semi-Custodial Penalties: Report of the Advisory Council on the Penal System* (1970). For authority to impose this sanction in this country, see, e.g., N.Y. Penal Law, art. 85 (authorizing sentences of "intermittent imprisonment").

4. See Home Office, *Custodial and Semi-Custodial Penalties, supra* note 3.

5. Ibid.

Chapter 15

1. For data on low recidivism rates among convicted murderers, see, e.g., National Council on Crime and Delinquency Research Center, "Parole Risk of Convicted Murderers," *Uniform Parole Reports Newsletter*, December 1972.

Chapter 16

1. A five-year limit has been suggested before, on the basis of more traditional theories of sentencing. See, e.g., American Bar Association, *Sentencing Alternatives and Procedures, supra* note 1 to Chapter 2, §2.1(d); NACCJSG, *Corrections*, Standard 5.2; *Model Sentencing Act*, §9.

2. For citations in footnote: James Q. Wilson, *Thinking about Crime* (New York: Basic Books, 1975), ch. 10; Shlomo and Reuel Shinnar, "A Simplified Model for Estimating the Effects of the Criminal Justice System on the Control of Crime," School of Engineering, City College of New York, 1974 (unpublished), cited in Wilson, *Thinking about Crime*.

For a different view of incapacitative effects, see David F. Greenberg, "The Incapacitative Effect of Imprisonment: Some Estimates," Department of Sociology, New York University, 1975 (unpublished).

3. For citation in footnote: Willard Gaylin, "Not for the Gander, Though," *New York Times*, May 21, 1975, p. 43.

4. For 1969 statistics on time of first release for various major-crime categories in California, see State of California, Department of Corrections, *California Prisoners, 1969* (Sacramento, Cal.: undated).

Part V

Chapter 17

1. H. L. A. Hart, "Prolegomenon," *supra* note 11 to Chapter 6, p. 15.
2. See, e.g., Joseph Goldstein, "The Brawner Rule—Why?, or No More Nonsense on Non Sense in the Criminal Law, Please!" 1973 *Washington University Law Quarterly* 126 (1973).

Appendix
Additional Views
of Individual
Committee Members

JOSEPH GOLDSTEIN

I AM in substantial support of the sentencing reforms outlined in the preface by Charles Goodell and attributed by him to the Committee's report. I share the report's reasons for rejecting as unjust and unworkable current sentencing policy which rests on meeting the "rehabilitative needs" of each convicted offender and which relies on trial judge and parole board to determine when an individual offender will be and is "rehabilitated" and thus safe for release from imprisonment. Even if such diagnostic and predictive powers were, as they are not, within anyone's competence, the assignment of such broad discretion to court and agency to fix the length of incarceration on a case-by-case basis is bound to lead, as it has, not only to a "runaway" inflation in the length of sentences but also to discrimination for the same crime in favor of the relatively well placed offender and against the already disadvantaged one.

Without precisely defined restraints on the power of the court

to incarcerate and on the power of those who administer
sentences to keep an offender in prison, one element critical to the
criminal law of a democratic society is missing—i.e., a guarantee
of fair warning of the consequences which will follow conviction
for a specific crime. Thus the report correctly concludes that the
authority to punish ought no longer be loosely left to court or
administrative agency discretion and that the severity of punishment is to be fixed in advance for each type of crime and is to
accord with society's notions of its seriousness. With the elimination of the discretion of the sentencer and the sentence administrator, incarceration will be imposed and will only be imposed for
a time certain in response to what the convicted offender has
done, not what someone "expects he will do if treated in a certain
fashion." Up to this point I am in substantial agreement with the
analysis and conclusions of the report and to that extent subscribe
to it.

However, in proposing that the *principle of commensurate
deserts* should become the guide to sentencing policy, the report
retreats from its own analysis and conclusions. It reintroduces—
albeit under another label—the traditional notions upon which
current sentencing systems are based. As interpreted by the
report, the deserts principle—which, by the way, is never
sufficiently clarified to become an operational guide for lawmak-
ers—invites the sentencing judge to take into account the prior
record and "mental state" of the offender.

The report, to give but one example of the confusion introduced by the deserts principle, argues: "A repetition of the
offense following [a prior] conviction may be regarded as more
culpable, since he persisted in the behavior after having been
forcefully censured for it through his prior punishment." This
thinly disguised throwback to individualization and concern for an
offender's "culpability"—i.e., failure to learn from (be reformed
by) punishment for his prior offense—undercuts much of the
report's most significant point, which is that in determining the
seriousness of an offense, and hence the severity of the punishment, focus must be on the crime committed, not the individual
who commits it. Further, the report urges that the amount of

"time passed since the previous conviction" should also be taken into account in setting the sentence. Why these and other (or, for that matter, not other) factors are to be considered in establishing the severity of the punishment under the deserts principle is never clarified.

But what does become clear is that the report is forced to rationalize the reintroduction of a potentially discriminating sentencing discretion for the court. And it backs away from concluding what its initial analysis would have dictated, which is that parole boards would no longer have a function in criminal-law administration. An offender would be released upon completion of a sentence fixed, not just for him, but for all persons who are convicted for the same crime. The sentence would have been predetermined by the legislature to provide punishment severe enough to reflect society's notions about the seriousness of the offense. But the report abandons that conclusion and moves full circle under the deserts principle to an abuse-prone discretionary sentencing system not unlike the one it so thoroughly discredited in its opening chapters. It recommends that there be a "presumptive sentence" for each offense and that judges be authorized "to raise the penalty above or reduce it below the presumptive sentence, in cases where he finds there were special circumstances affecting the gravity of the violation and where he specifies what those circumstances of aggravation or mitigation were." Nothing in the *principle of commensurate deserts* gives guidance to sentencing judges and courts of review—let alone all of us who are subject to the criminal law—concerning the certainty or the appropriateness of a judge's "specifics" for increasing or reducing the presumptive—no longer fixed—sentence.

I do not suggest that legislatures should not provide, for example, fixed increments in the length of sentences to be imposed upon offenders who repeat offenses, even to the point of long-term incarcerations for those who repeat or repeatedly engage in the most serious crimes. But such terms would be fixed in advance by legislative decision. As the sentencing power of judges is thus restrained, the critical element of fair warning would be preserved. Of course, it must be recognized that a specific type of crime does not cause less or more serious harm because in one case it is the work of a first offender and in another that of a third offender. The more severe, though fixed, punishments, for example, would be justified, not because of some "moral claim" (whose source and meaning are never revealed in the report's discussions of the principle of commensurate deserts), but possibly because the legislature is less willing to assume the "additional" risk of having any repeaters at large and/or because the legislature wishes to reflect the exacerbation of society's retributive feelings toward recidivists.

Furthermore, the report fails to acknowledge that an inescapable and critical function of the criminal law is to satisfy and to channel the retributive feelings aroused by those who offend. Retribution, whether we like it or not, must be a factor in any calculation of seriousness of harm and of severity of punishment. But the report makes the deserts principle, not unlike the rehabilitative ideal, a cover for retribution and vengeance. It creates just another discretionary sentencing system with a new and protean slogan for justifying retributive excesses under a vaguely articulated "moral claim," in place of a "do-gooder" claim to cure the sick offender. Thus, I join Gaylin and Rothman, who in their introduction observe: "When we honestly face the fact that our purpose is retributive, we may, with a re-found compassion and a renewed humanity, limit the degree of retribution we will exact." Unfortunately, the report neither faces that fact nor provides that hope in its proffer of the commensurate-deserts principle.

Finally, the report does not give sufficient focus to living conditions in institutions of incarceration. Nor does the deserts principle give guidance to the management of such punishments. Further, insufficient emphasis is placed on the application of the criminal law to conduct within prisons, especially with respect to punishing crimes committed by prison administrators against incarcerated offenders. The report does not adequately develop the notion that prisoners should not be deprived of any rights or safeguards to which a person on the outside is entitled, unless such deprivations further the acknowledged purposes of the punishment.

SIMON ROTTENBERG

I SUBSCRIBE to the Committee report because I believe it comes to the right conclusion, but I think it does so for the wrong reasons.

I start from libertarian and utilitarian premises.

I believe that the exercise of power produces mischief and that the state, which possesses the ultimate authority of coercion, is an instrument of power and therefore an instrument of mischief.

I think that the state and its agents ought to be constrained.

It ought to intrude minimally, and only when provocation is severe, into the lives of the citizenry.

The intrusion of the state appears in one of its sharpest forms when it selects out members of the community for punishment and when it punishes them.

Imprisonment is an especially strong and pernicious form of punishment because it puts convicted persons at the mercy of wardens and guards who administer power by enforcing rules governing even the most trivial aspects of the lives and behavior of prisoners.

The libertarian premise instructs me that the state not infrequently punishes behavior it ought to tolerate and that it often punishes by imprisoning when alternatives are available that would imply the exercise of less power by the state's agents.

This is not to say that the state should never punish or that punishment should never take the form of imprisonment.

For instruction on the definition of the conditions in which the state *should* intrude, I look to the utilitarian premise.

Sometimes the behavior of some does harm to others. We shall be happier if the quantity of harm done is smaller, rather than larger. The quantity of harm done will be diminished if costs are imposed upon harm-doers; we observe cost avoidance as a behavioral motivator in many facets of life.

Costs can be imposed upon harm-doers either by making them the objects of civil suit in which those who are harmed take the initiative to cause harm-doers to be compelled to "make them whole," or by the mobilization of the resources of the state to prosecute criminals.

Which of these is the more appropriate will depend on the kind of harm wrought and on which is cheaper in terms of the real resources employed to diminish harm by some quantity.

For those classes of harmful behavior which should appropriately trigger the state's intrusion, costs should be imposed upon those who have done criminal harm to the point where the last unit of resources used in punishing has a value to society that is equal to the social value of the harm it forestalls.

Punishment by the state is equivalent to making criminal harm-doing more costly for the criminal. Less harm will therefore be done. All this implies that the punishment to be expected by a criminal should be proportional to the degree of seriousness of the criminal harm he does.

That is to say, I think the whole acceptable rationale for punishment is general deterrence.

I believe this the only respect in which punishment is socially useful.

I believe this rationale suffices as the defense for punishment and that it is unnecessary and mischievous in logic and effect to introduce the principle of desert to buttress that defense.

Wherever punishment can be transformed from imprisonment to some other form that reduces the power of the agents of the state but leaves undiminished the magnitude of cost felt by wrongdoers, non-incarcerative punishments should be levied.

Imprisonment is appropriate only as a last resort, when alternative forms of punishment will not do. And punishment by the state is appropriate only when it is socially less expensive than civil remedies and only when it will diminish the harm done.

The magnitudes of punishments for different offenses are appropriately defined by the resource cost to society of executing them and the gain to society in forestalled criminal harm.

I must add, finally, that I disassociate myself from the implications of the seventeenth chapter on "just deserts in an unjust society."

I think the ideas there expressed, explicitly and especially implicitly, are, for the most part, abysmally wrong. I am at loss to understand how they could have been generated by a committee such as this, which was characterized by intelligence and erudition.

HERMAN SCHWARTZ

I DO not believe the deserts principle should serve as one of the principal rationales for a system of punishment. Can one really say that someone *deserves* to be punished for breaking the law, when that person may have been hooked on heroin by the time he was a teenager, was confronted with racism or other prejudice, grew up in a broken home amid violence, filth, and brutality, was forced to go to substandard schools, and had no honest way to make a decent living? Those conditions apply to a very high percentage of our criminal population. I would limit the deserts principle to serving as a guide to the distribution of punishment (only those who commit crime may be punished) and perhaps as a rough criterion for the level of punishment, e.g., no heavy punishments for minor offenses or token sanctions for major crimes.

With these reservations, I join in the report, both in general and in its specific recommendations.

LESLIE T. WILKINS

I CANNOT do other than add my signature to this report, but I do so without enthusiasm: my difficulty is not with the report but rather with the situation it reflects. Had it been possible for a different model to apply—economic/rational or even humanitarian/therapeutic—I would have preferred it: but such models have proven still less appropriate. It seems that we have rediscovered "sin," in the absence of a better alternative!

The simplification of the problem of crime to the problem of the criminal has not paid off, and we in this report are still forced into oversimplifications of the issues of effective social control. We may have said something about what should be done with criminals, but we have added nothing to suggestions for dealing with crime.

I am content that the statement we have made serves as an interim declaration of policy. I cannot accept it as a declaration of a desirable policy—it is merely less unacceptable than any others which can be considered at this time. I would stress, therefore, the need for continuous review by research methods of the workings of the criminal-justice processes and, in particular, the sentencing procedures of the courts. We should link with exploratory research those methods which require controlled variation of the processes in operational terms. The variation would serve two purposes. Any system which cannot tolerate variation has already ossified. We desire equity, but not rigidity. Variation is essential in order to generate information, and information is necessary to indicate how progress may be achieved. There is a moral necessity for man to attempt to know more and more, even about man himself, even if this incurs some cost.

I do not think the report gives adequate emphasis to the need for experimentation, perhaps because it takes a thoroughly moralistic model. I do not disagree with that viewpoint, provided that the need to research into moral values is itself seen as a moral imperative. The moral perspective may devalue research because it reduces the importance of arguments about efficiency (such as resource-allocation problems) by dismissing these as "economic issues." I would not agree—every technical problem implies a moral problem, but we have few proven techniques for research into the latter.

The practice of parole and its philosophy is, of course, open to challenge insofar as it is based upon the idea of "treatment." Parole boards, however, can act as sentencing-review bodies and

would seem to be capable of developing high levels of competence in this form of decision-making. Certainly, the United States
Board of Parole (federal) was the first criminal-justice agency to
adopt a procedure not dissimilar to that advocated in the report.
They have (as the report notes) adopted guidelines (based on
research) for decisions setting the time inmates are held in prison
before release on parole. The guidelines give most weight to the
rated seriousness of the instant offense, with some additional
weight to other factors, mainly classifications of the prior criminal
record or its correlates. The times indicated by the guidelines may
be departed from, but reasons for departure must be given.
Inmates are informed of the reasons for decisions and they have
access to various methods of appeal, both through administrative
processes and through the courts. Review of the policy coded into
the guidelines is facilitated by the appeal procedures, the analysis
of reasons for departures from the indicated times, and by other
statistical analyses. The board meets at regular intervals to
consider these data and to ratify or modify the procedures
accordingly. Of course, all persons about whom decisions are
made by the Board of Parole have served some time in incarceration, whereas, in sentencing, the major determination to be made
is with respect to "in" or "out." Nonetheless, some of the phrasing
of the report does not seem (to my biased viewpoint) to give
sufficient credit to the U.S. Board of Parole for adopting a
revolutionary philosophy and implementing it in practice for
assessing the time convicted offenders should serve in prison.